SUBSCRIBE!!

GET THE ULTIMATE SOURCE
ANIME, MANGA A...

URBANA FREE LIBRARY

Newtype USA 米国版

THE MOVING PICTURES MAGAZINE

FEB
2005
VOLUME 04
NUMBER 02

FREE DVD!
2 FULL EPISODES
SUBTITLED & DUBBED
SPECIAL MANGA INSERT
MONTHLY COLOR
CENTERFOLD!

...GUIDE
Secrets from the
house that Miyazaki built

DON'T BUY
ANOTHER DVD
...until you read our
in-depth reviews of
all the latest anime!

VALENTINE
SPECIAL

Gantz
MADLAX
D·N·Angel
Saiyuki Reload
Samurai Champloo
Fullmetal Alche...
PLUS! 8 MOR...
HOT FEATURI...

DATE DUE		

WORLD
EXCLUSI...

FIRST...

DVD,
INSERT
D
ERFOLD
ER
SSUE!!

Go to www.n...
get a full year (12 issues) for
over 50% off the cover price!

日刊ニュータイプ
type USA 米国版

THE MOVING PICTURES MAGAZINE.

www.newtype-usa.com

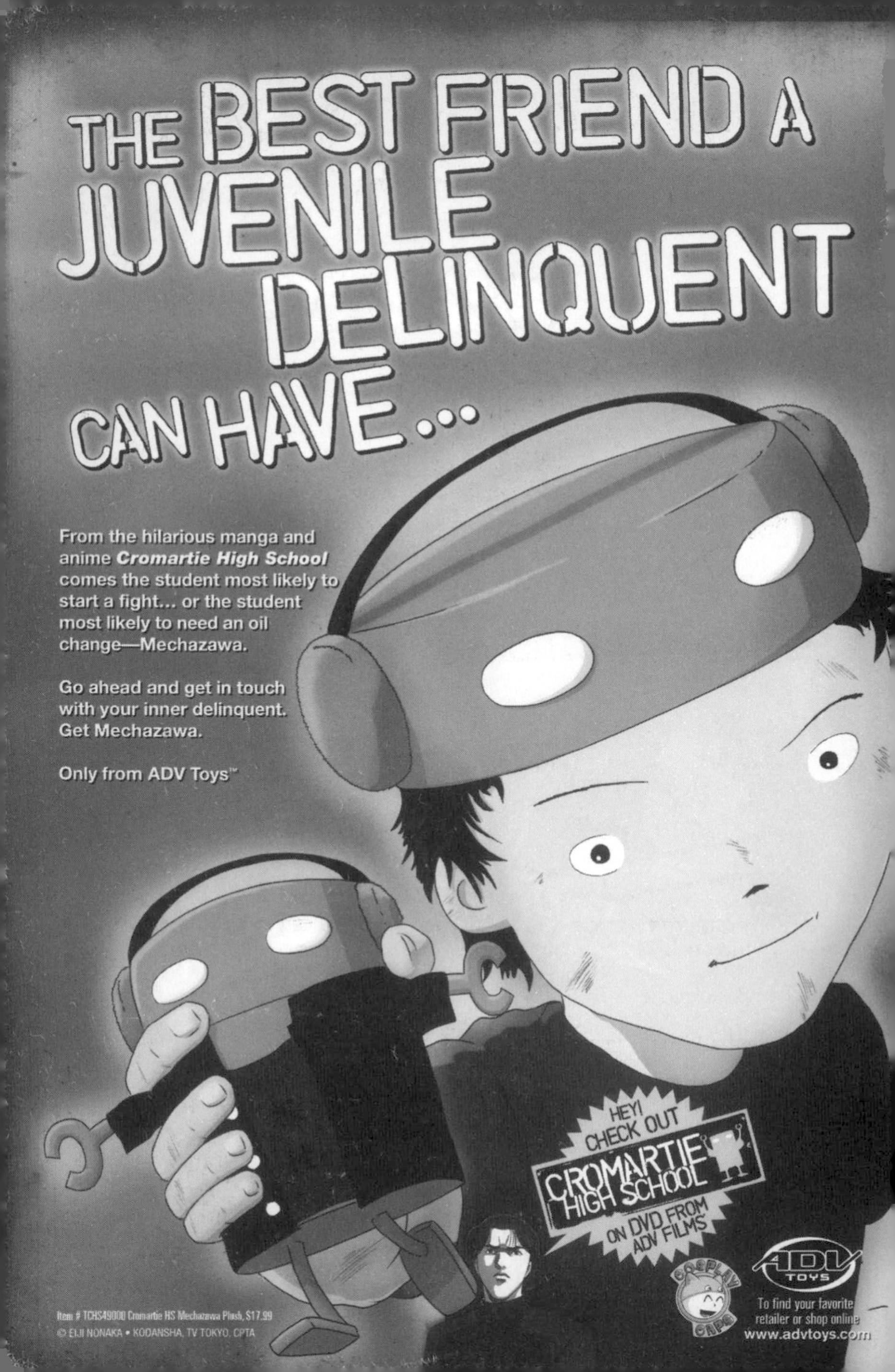
THE BEST FRIEND A JUVENILE DELINQUENT CAN HAVE...
From the hilarious manga and anime Cromartie High School comes the student most likely to start a fight... or the student most likely to need an oil change—Mechazawa.
Go ahead and get in touch with your inner delinquent. Get Mechazawa.
Only from ADV Toys™
HEY! CHECK OUT
CROMARTIE HIGH SCHOOL
ON DVD FROM ADV FILMS
COSPLAY CAPS
ADV TOYS
To find your favorite retailer or shop online
www.advtoys.com
Item # TCHS49000 Cromartie HS Mechazawa Plush, $17.99
© EIJI NONAKA • KODANSHA, TV TOKYO, CPTA

CROMARTIE HIGH SCHOOL

JAPAN'S #1 COMEDY IS GUARANTEED TO MAKE YOU A FRIGGIN' GENIUS*

SPECIAL OFFER!
Vol. 1 DVD + Collector's Box comes with Volume 1 of the *Cromartie High School* and **Bonus Manga!** GET IT WHILE YOU CAN! IT'S JAM-PACKED WITH EVEN MORE IDIOTS!

*Compared to all the freakin' morons at Cromartie High School, anyone could be considered a genius. Come on, do you know ANYONE who would eat an entire box of pencils at once?! THE WHOLE BOX IN ONE BITE! Like FIFTY PENCILS! Yeah, didn't think so. Also, this one guy... he's not a guy at all... he's a **FREAKING ROBOT!** They all think he's a **DUDE!** Don't even ask about the Gorilla... or that one dude Freddie... He looks really, really familiar...

BUY IT!
VOL. 1 DVD CROMARTIAN RHAPSODY

WANNA LEARN HOW TO BE A REAL BADASS?
Tips on how to be a real juvenile delinquent in the first volume of the *Cro-High* manga!
GRAB IT!

LIMITED EDITION MECHAZAWA PLUSH
$17.99

EDITOR'S
PICKS

IF YOU LIKE *CROMARTIE HIGH SCHOOL*, THEN YOU'LL LOVE THESE!

PICK 1

AZUMANGA DAIOH

It's not manga, it's Azumanga! Created by Kiyohiko Azuma, the madcap genius behind *YOTSUBA&!*, *Azumanga Daioh* is smart, funny and totally out of control! Featuring kooky characters who meander through their everyday lives, it takes the reader through the daily tribulations of Miss Kurosawa, Miss Yukari, the wild Tomo, hair-triggered Yomi, ditzy Osaka, brash Kagura, cute Chiyo-chan and sporty Sakaki. It's seriously silly, and completely addictive!

© KIYOHIKO AZUMA 2000

PICK 2

RAY

Ray is a grown woman with a troubled past and a superhuman gift— X-ray vision! Raised on an organ-donor farm, her own eyes were taken and sold on the black market. When she unexpectedly became the recipient of a new set of bionic eyes, Ray found that she could once again see the world...and a lot more of it! Now, working as a nurse and moonlighting as a surgeon-for-hire, Ray is ready to face her past and bring down the underground group that robbed her of her childhood.

© Akihito Yoshitomi/Akitashoten 2003

PICK 3

ORPHEN

Orphen, the tough-talking sorcerer-for-hire, is putting his wand-wielding skills to use for a price, but with a boneheaded companion and a wide-eyed pupil tagging along, they can't help but attract a little trouble! Magical mercenaries are all around, and the hair-triggered Orphen is no stranger to a good fight, so he'll have to cast his spells in record time to stay in the game of magic!

© 1998 Yoshinobu Akita/Hajime Sawada
© 1998 Yuuya Kusaka

OUT NOW FROM ADV MANGA!

www.adv-manga.com

The real Takenouchi has finally made it back
to Japan, despite his motion sickness...
to Japan, despite his motion sickness...
but his stomach-turning travels
have just begun!

It's time for the Cromartie school trip, and
armed with a plastic bag, he's determined to
conquer his most fearsome rival yet
—the bullet train!

Continued...

Pg. 41

Wonderful Girls

The television show *Wonderful* ran from October 1997 to September 2002 on the TBS network. Billed as a "variety show," the program's main draw was its panel of 12 young models and aspiring actresses, to which the camera would frequently cut away for reaction (and zoom) shots. Following the publication of this volume of *Cromartie High School*, there was actually a *fifth* cast rotation, the final batch of Wonderful Girls being chosen from over 500 hopefuls.

Pg. 90

Mil Máscaras

Born Aaron Rodriguez, Mil Máscaras (lit. "Thousand Masks") is a professional Mexican wrestler known for, as one would imagine, his wide variety of costumes. He would go on to international fame, capturing the WWA World Heavyweight Title and WCWA World Tag Team Title.

Pg. 108

(1) Ken Takakura

A staple of the Japanese film industry, the tough guy who's been everything from a hardened cop *(Black Rain)* to a stationmaster *(Poppoya*, aka "Railroad Man"). Quentin Tarantino paid a brief homage to Takakura in the script for *Pulp Fiction* when he wrote that Bruce Willis's character wielded his samurai sword "Takakura Ken-style."

(2) Koji Tsuruta

Another old-school tough guy, Tsuruta's earlier roles were mostly period pieces such as *Chushingura* and the *Samurai* films (starring screen legend Toshiro Mifune). He would later appear in dozens of hard-boiled crime films throughout the 60s and 70s.

Pg. 111

Baseball and shaved heads

Japanese little leaguers tend to have shaved heads, hence Hayashida's rather offbeat suggestion.

Pg. 141

Hidden ball trick

A baseball technique wherein the pitcher (or an infielder) pretends to not have the ball in order to tag unsuspecting runners.

Pg. 155

Osamu Tezuka

Known in Japan as the "god of manga," this legendary artist is responsible for such landmark titles as *Astroboy*, *Blackjack* and *Kimba the White Lion*.

Pg. 156

Tone

"Tone" refers to what some manga artists use to create gradation in shading and for background elements such as clouds and water. It usually comes in thin sheets of paper which must be precisely cut—resulting in small scraps that can get all over the place.

Cromartie High School Vol. 03

PG. 1   Masks

In this distinctly *Cromartie*-esque family portrait, the kanji character appearing on all three foreheads is the *take* (lit. "bamboo") in the family name Takenouchi.

PG. 19   The Two Beats

While "Beat" Takeshi Kitano has gained international fame as an actor/director in such films as *Brother* and *Zatoichi*, his initial break in show business came as part of the brash comedy duo "The Two Beats," in which he was joined by fellow "Beat" Kiyoshi. The two parted ways in the early 1980s.

PG. 20   (1) Koshien baseball championship

This annual high school playoff draws its name from the venue in which it is held, the Hanshin Koshien Stadium in Nishinomiya, Japan. Its popularity is universal, rivaling that of the Super Bowl in the United States.

(2) Antonio Inoki

One of the most famous Japanese pro wrestlers of all time. In June 1976, he fought a 15-round bout against boxing superstar Muhammad Ali that ended in a draw.

PG. 21   *Zaibatsu*

The *zaibatsu* are large Japanese conglomerates whose origins go back hundreds of years. These companies gained considerable social and political power, especially in the early 1900s, and many are still around today. The supposed "big four" of the *zaibatsu* are Mitsubishi, Mitsui, Sumitomo, and Yasuda (but don't tell that to The Hokuto Foundation).

PG. 22   Hokkaido and bears

Hokkaido is the northernmost of Japan's main four islands. Its wide open plains lend it a kind of "frontier" image within Japan—one that is compounded by the number of bears on the island.

CROMARTIE HIGH SCHOOL VOLUME THREE

© 2001 Eiji Nonaka
All rights reserved.
First published in Japan in 2001 by Kodansha Ltd., Tokyo
English translation rights for this edition arranged through Kodansha Ltd.

Editor **JAVIER LOPEZ**
Translator **BRENDAN FRAYNE**
Assistant Editor **SHERIDAN JACOBS**
Graphic Artists **NATALIA REYNOLDS, MARK MEZA**

Editorial Director **GARY STEINMAN**
Creative Director **JASON BABLER**
Print Production Manager **BRIDGETT JANOTA**
Sales and Marketing **CHRIS OARR**
Production Coordinator **MARISA KREITZ**

International Coordinators **TORU IWAKAMI, MIYUKI KAMIYA AND AI TAKAI**

President, CEO & Publisher **JOHN LEDFORD**

Email: editor@adv-manga.com
www.adv-manga.com
www.advfilms.com

For sales and distribution inquiries please call 1.800.282.7202

is a division of A.D. Vision, Inc.
5750 Bintliff Drive, Suite 210, Houston, Texas 77036

English text © 2005 published by A.D. Vision, Inc. under exclusive license.
ADV MANGA is a trademark of A.D. Vision, Inc.

ISBN: 1-4139-0259-6
First printing, August 2005
10 9 8 7 6 5 4 3 2 1
Printed in Canada

Afterword:

Uh...

I don't really like
manga that much.

BETTER NOT ASK NONA FOR HELP.

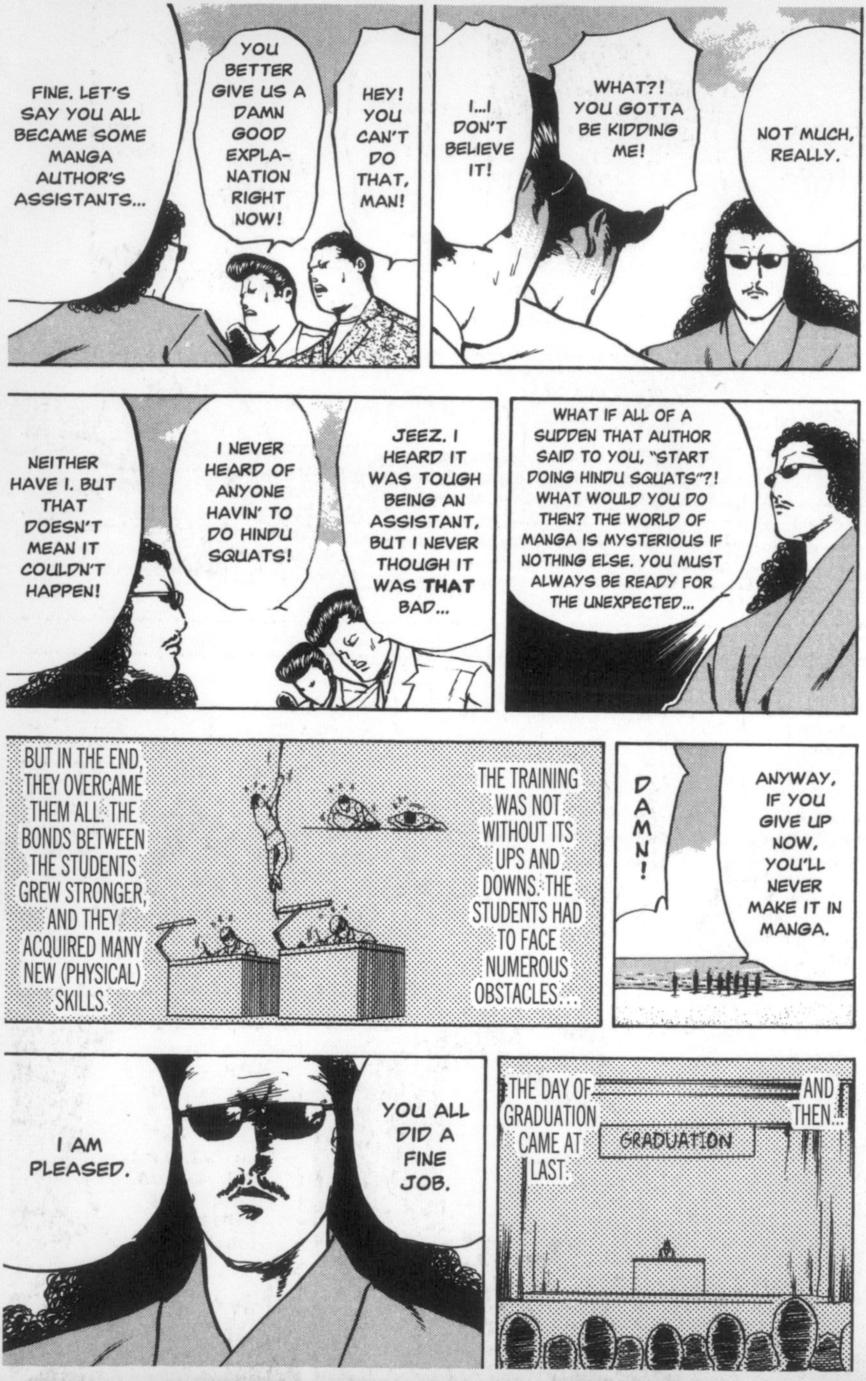
NOT MUCH, REALLY.
WHAT?! YOU GOTTA BE KIDDING ME!
I...I DON'T BELIEVE IT!
HEY! YOU CAN'T DO THAT, MAN!
YOU BETTER GIVE US A DAMN GOOD EXPLANATION RIGHT NOW!
FINE. LET'S SAY YOU ALL BECAME SOME MANGA AUTHOR'S ASSISTANTS...
WHAT IF ALL OF A SUDDEN THAT AUTHOR SAID TO YOU, "START DOING HINDU SQUATS"?! WHAT WOULD YOU DO THEN? THE WORLD OF MANGA IS MYSTERIOUS IF NOTHING ELSE. YOU MUST ALWAYS BE READY FOR THE UNEXPECTED...
JEEZ. I HEARD IT WAS TOUGH BEING AN ASSISTANT, BUT I NEVER THOUGH IT WAS THAT BAD...
I NEVER HEARD OF ANYONE HAVIN' TO DO HINDU SQUATS!
NEITHER HAVE I. BUT THAT DOESN'T MEAN IT COULDN'T HAPPEN!
ANYWAY, IF YOU GIVE UP NOW, YOU'LL NEVER MAKE IT IN MANGA.
DAMN!
THE TRAINING WAS NOT WITHOUT ITS UPS AND DOWNS. THE STUDENTS HAD TO FACE NUMEROUS OBSTACLES...
BUT IN THE END, THEY OVERCAME THEM ALL. THE BONDS BETWEEN THE STUDENTS GREW STRONGER, AND THEY ACQUIRED MANY NEW (PHYSICAL) SKILLS.
AND THEN...
THE DAY OF GRADUATION CAME AT LAST.
GRADUATION
YOU ALL DID A FINE JOB.
I AM PLEASED.

SOMEBODY... WATER, PLEASE!

I CAN'T RUN ANYMORE.

I... I CAN'T DO IT!

YOU WANTED WATER, RIGHT? WELL DRINK UP!

WHAT DID YOU DO THAT FOR?!

GRGH!

SPLASH

DISCOURAGED ALREADY?! HMPH! THERE'S NO **WAY** I CAN LET YOU HOLD A PEN AND PAPER YET!

AT LEAST LET US DO SOME SKETCHES!

YEAH! LET US APPLY SOME SCREEN TONE ALREADY, YA BASTARD!

WHEN ARE YOU GONNA GIVE US A PEN OR SOMETHIN'?!

HEY! WHY DO YOU GOT US DOIN' ALL THIS STUFF? I THOUGHT WE CAME HERE TO DRAW MANGA!

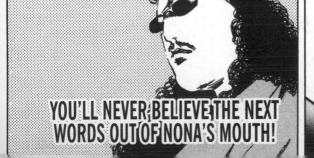

YOU'LL NEVER BELIEVE THE NEXT WORDS OUT OF NONA'S MOUTH!

HEY, NONA-SENSEI! CAN I ASK YOU A QUESTION? WHAT DOES ALL THIS TRAINING HAVE TO DO WITH MANGA ANYWAY?

WHAT WAS THAT?!

HAH! **YOU'RE** THE ONES WHO DON'T KNOW ANYTHING!

DON'T YOU KNOW ANYTHING ABOUT MANGA?!

A MANGA THAT TELLS A FRICKIN' STORY! THERE'S LOTS OF KINDS OF MANGA, YOU KNOW! WHAT, DID YOU THINK THERE WAS ONLY COMEDY?

UH...OF COURSE!

DOES THIS MEAN EVEN OSAMU TEZUKA STARTED OUT DOING GAG MANGA?!

HUH?

ALL COMIC ARTISTS GET THEIR START BY DRAWING "GAG MANGA." IT'S THE LAW OF THE MANGA WORLD! IF YOU BREAK IT, YOU'LL NEVER MAKE YOUR PROFESSIONAL DEBUT-- HECK, YOU'LL NEVER EVEN GET IN WITH THE PUBLISHERS!

YOU'LL ALL HAVE TO START FROM SCRATCH.

DAMN! I DREW AN EPIC ROMANCE!

Uh, he ain't a manga artist.

WHOA, SPIELBERG DID GAG MANGA?!

AND NOT JUST OSAMU TEZUKA. TETSUO HARA, TAKEHIKO INOUE... EVEN STEVEN SPIELBERG! THEY ALL STARTED OUT DOING GAG MANGA!

COME ON! PUT SOME ENERGY INTO IT, PEOPLE!

ONE, TWO! ONE, TWO!

COME WITH ME.

NORMALLY I WOULDN'T BE CAUGHT READING SUCH AN *AMATEUR* WORK.

HMPH! THEY SAY THE SMALLEST DOGS BARK LOUDEST.

HERE! READ MY FRICKIN' MANGA!

CRAP! IF A GUY THIS TALENTED EVER MAKES IT BIG, IT'LL THREATEN MY POSITION AS A MANGA AUTHOR! I'D BETTER NIP THIS ONE IN THE BUD, AND FAST.

THIS IS *GOOD!*

IF YOU ASK ME, THIS THING'S NOTHING BUT TRASH. HELL, IT'S **LESS** THAN TRASH!

WHAT THE HELL ARE YOU DOIN'?!

rrrip

A WHAT?

DUDE, THAT WAS A STORY MANGA!

UH, PUNCH-LINE?

FOR STARTERS, THAT PUNCHLINE WAS WEAK! YOU THINK READERS WOULD LAUGH AT **THAT**?

PLEASE, DON'T SAY THINGS LIKE THAT! THIS IS A **PRODUCTION**.

SO...IS THIS ALL STAGED?

CAN I ASK YOU SOME-THING?

GOT IT.

AND YOU WITH THE DUCKTAIL, SHOUT A LITTLE MORE FIERCELY, OK?

HEY! QUIT YOUR BLABBIN' AND START THE DAMN LESSON!

UH, WHY DON'T WE ALL START BY INTRO-DUCING...

AND... ACTION!

HEARIN' YOU TALK DOWN TO ME LIKE THAT REALLY PISSES ME OFF!

THAT'S WHAT TV IS ALL ABOUT.

DAMN STRAIGHT! WE'RE HERE TO DRAW MANGA!

SHUT YER HOLE! WE DIDN'T COME HERE TO LEARN NO MANNERS!

HMPH! WHAT YOU KIDS NEED TO LEARN EVEN MORE THAN MANGA ARE SOME **MANNERS**.

THE THING IS, DO YOU PUNKS HAVE WHAT IT TAKES TO EVEN DRAW A **GOOD** MANGA?

WELL...IN THIS DAY AND AGE, I GUESS IT DOESN'T MATTER IF YOU'VE GOT A BAD ATTITUDE OR A LOUSY PERSONALITY. AS LONG AS YOU CAN DO A GOOD COMIC, THAT SEEMS TO BE ENOUGH.

BUT YOU'RE GONNA HAVE A HARD TIME GETTING **THESE** GUYS TO DRAW ANYTHING!

HEINOUS MANGA IS THE WAY TO GO! BUT CAN DELINQUENTS REALLY DRAW?!

CEMENT!! MANGA CLUB

WHOA! WHAT AN AMAZINGLY BAD ATTITUDE!

HEY, QUIT FLAPPIN' YOUR LIPS. LET'S GET THIS DAMN THING **STARTED!**

SORRY. GUESS I'M JUST NOT USED TO IT YET.

MR. NONA, YOU'RE SUPPOSED TO BE AN INSTRUCTOR! PLEASE TRY TO SPEAK WITH MORE **AUTHORITY.**

HUH?

CUT!

CONNOISSEUR OF MANGA THAT I AM, I HAVE CREATED A SERIES TITLED "TOOTHPICK HIGH SCHOOL," WHICH IS NOW RUNNING SERIALLY. AS A SIDE NOTE, IT HASN'T BEEN MET WITH MUCH SUCCESS...

I AM COMEDY MANGA AUTHOR EIJI NONA (P/S - I'M SINGLE).

A GROUP OF RESENTFUL DELINQUENTS GET TOGETHER ONLY TO FIND A NEW PURPOSE AND MEANING IN THEIR LIVES. IT'S A SHOW ABOUT TURNING OVER NEW LEAVES, ABOUT REALIZING YOUR GOALS AND AMBITIONS.

TELL ME ABOUT THE PROGRAM, AND MAKE IT SNAPPY!

I'M HAYA-SHIDA, THE EDITOR.

BUT THAT DIDN'T STOP ME FROM BEING ASKED TO APPEAR ON A TV SHOW!

AH. I THINK I GET THE GIST OF IT...

THE THEME FOR EACH EPISODE WILL RANGE FROM BOXING TO BIKE RACES. IT'S ALREADY BEING CALLED A VERY POSITIVE SHOW.

THE POLICE

MANGA I DREW
IN FIVE MINUTES

MANGA I DREW
IN FIVE MINUTES

SO ENDS YOUR TRAINING.

shove

TRASH
(Non-burnables)

bwshhh

BE EVER DILIGENT, MY PUPIL.

THANK YOU, MASTER.

BUT WHY DID HE HAVE TO THROW HIM AWAY?!

AND SHOULDN'T IT HAVE GONE WITH THE BURNABLES?

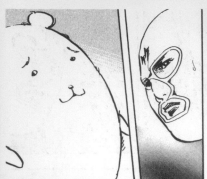

I'VE GROWN TO LOVE THIS STUFFED ANIMAL! HE'S LIKE A BROTHER TO ME! I'M SORRY, BUT I CAN'T HIT HIM. I RESIGN FROM PILLOW-JUTSU.

I...I CAN'T DO IT!

clatter

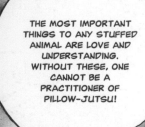

THE MOST IMPORTANT THINGS TO ANY STUFFED ANIMAL ARE LOVE AND UNDERSTANDING. WITHOUT THESE, ONE CANNOT BE A PRACTITIONER OF PILLOW-JUTSU!

HUH?!

WELL DONE. YOU PASS.

THANK YOU, MASTER!

YES. I NAME **YOU** AS MY SUC-CESSOR.

YOU MEAN...

WE ATE MEALS TOGETHER...

THE ANSWER ELUDED ME, SO I DECIDED TO SPEND ALL MY TIME WITH THE STUFFED ANIMAL.

I USED IT AS A SPONGE.

WE EVEN TOOK BATHS TOGETHER.

WE PLAYED TOGETHER...

REMEMBER-- THIS TIME I WILL NOT TOLERATE FAILURE.

ONE WEEK LATER

BEFORE I KNEW IT, A BOND HAD FORMED BETWEEN US. WE HAD BECOME ONE.

Y-YES, MASTER.

NOW TRY AGAIN!

I-IT'S NOT SOFT AT ALL! IF ANYTHING, IT'S EVEN **HARDER**!

WHAT'S WRONG?

I'M SURE IT WILL BE NICE AND...

I WILL GIVE YOU ONE LAST CHANCE. SEVEN DAYS FROM NOW, YOU WILL TRY AGAIN. IF YOU FAIL...YOU WILL BE BANISHED FROM THIS ART!

FOOL! **PRIDE** IS THE SOURCE OF YOUR FAILURE! THIS IS NO NORMAL PILLOW!

TAKE-NOUCHI'S HOUSE

NO. YOU MUST FIND THE ANSWER ON YOUR OWN.

BUT MASTER, WHAT SHOULD I DO?! HELP ME TO UNDERSTAND!

IT'S NOT LIKE THIS GUY CAN TELL ME ANYTHING...

WHAT THE HECK AM I GOING TO DO?

YES, A STUFFED ANIMAL. IN A WAY, IT IS THE ULTIMATE PILLOW! MAKING THIS SOFT IS A MOST DIFFICULT TASK INDEED--ONE THAT REPRESENTS THE PINNACLE OF PILLOW-JUTSU!

DO THIS, AND YOU WILL BE CONSIDERED A MASTER.

A STUFFED ANIMAL?!

HYA!

swp

I DON'T WISH TO CONTRADICT YOU, BUT MY SKILLS IN PILLOW-JUTSU ARE FORMIDABLE. I DOUBT THIS WILL PRESENT MUCH OF A CHALLENGE.

WHY DON'T **YOU** TOUCH IT FIRST?

HERE.

fwap

fwap

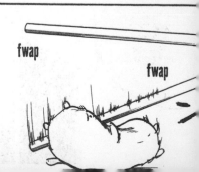

I SEE. IF YOU HAVE COME TO REALIZE THIS, THEN I HAVE NOTHING MORE TO TEACH YOU.

THERE IS ONE FINAL SECRET I MUST REVEAL TO YOU.

I AM OLD NOW, AND CHILDLESS. AS MY LAST PUPIL, **YOU** SHALL CARRY ON THE TRADITION OF PILLOW-JUTSU.

WHAT DO YOU MEAN?

YES, MASTER.

WAIT INSIDE.

OPEN IT.

THMP

THMP

FWAP

FWAP

AH. IT IS SOFT.

WELL?

MASTER, I'VE COMMITTED UNSPEAKABLE CRIMES IN MY LIFE. I'VE LIVED IN THE SHADOWS, TORMENTED BY MY SINS AND FEARFUL OF THE PUBLIC EYE.

BUT EVER SINCE I DISCOVERED PILLOW-JUTSU, I FEEL LIKE I'VE FOUND MY PLACE IN LIFE.

CHAPTER SEVENTY: **THE BITTEREST PILLOW**

YEAH, BUT I STILL THINK HOKUTO SUCKS AT BUNTING.

HMM. A VALUABLE LESSON.

THIS IS CALLED THE "HIDDEN BALL TRICK." IT'S A TECHNIQUE USED EVEN BY PROFESSIONAL PLAYERS.

IN THIS WAY, YOU WOULD BE ABLE TO TAG A RUNNER OUT.

NO. I HAVE **TRAINING** TODAY.

WORK?

SORRY GUYS, BUT I HAVE TO GET GOING.

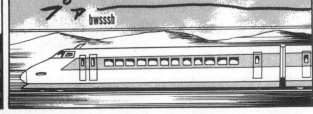

bwsssh

WHO ON EARTH COULD HAVE DONE THIS?

EVEN MAEDA.

THEY'RE ALL ASLEEP.

I DON'T KNOW WHO YOU ARE, BUT YOU'RE CERTAINLY A BIG HELP!

HYA!

fwap

THE SAGA OF PILLOW-JUTSU SHALL CONTINUE.

THEY AIN'T GONNA BE NO DIFFERENT FROM BEFORE. I OUGHTA SMASH YOUR FACE IN...

IF YOU PUT YOUR FACE UP ON IT, IT MAKES YOU WANNA GO TO SLEEP!

BUT IT WAS ALL HARD BEFORE! HOW DID THIS THING GET SO DAMN SOFT?!

IT...IT'S SOFT! LIKE A FRICKIN' MARSHMALLOW OR SOMETHIN'!

WHAT'S WRONG?

WHAT THE HELL?! IT'S LIKE ALL THESE YEARS I'VE BEEN SLEEPIN' ON A ROCK! **THIS** IS A REAL PILLOW!

THEY MIGHT'VE KILLED HIM ALREADY!

AT ANY RATE, WE'D BETTER HURRY BACK BEFORE THEY KILL MAEDA-KUN.

"TAKE ONE," HE SAYS! I'LL SHOW YOU, YA BASTARD!

HUH?!

EACH OF YOU TAKE ONE.

YOU SEE THESE PILLOWS?

YOU CAN'T GET NO GOOD NIGHT'S SLEEP ON THIS, YOU ASSHOLE!

This thing sucks!

MY PILLOW AT HOME IS WAY MORE COMFORTABLE THAN THIS!

WHAT THE HELL?! IT'S HARD AS A ROCK!

NOW TELL ME HOW THEY FEEL.

GIVE ME THAT!

YEAH, YOU'RE GONNA PAY FOR THIS!

YOU'RE ONE BOSSY SON OF A BITCH!

NOW THEN. LAY THOSE PILLOWS FLAT ON THE GROUND.

YOU'RE ASKIN' FOR IT, DIPSHIT!

TRY IT NOW.

HYAARGH!

fwap

fwap

URGH

I OUGHTA FINISH YOU OFF RIGHT NOW!

CHAPTER SIXTY-NINE:
BEAT SURRENDER

RGH!

LOOKS LIKE YOUR FRIENDS AIN'T COMIN' TO HELP YA, HUH?

HUH?

HOLD IT!

YOU THINK YOU CAN TAKE ALL OF US ON?!

WHO THE HELL ARE YOU?

HE'S BEEN STOLEN!

OVER TIME, I'VE COME TO THINK OF MECHAZAWA AS A FRIEND...

HOW STUPID OF ME! I SHOULD HAVE USED AT LEAST TWO CHAINS!

WELL, I'VE HEARD THAT BIKE THEFTS HAVE BEEN ON THE RISE.

FILE A MISSING PROPERTY REPORT, I SUPPOSE.

WHAT SHOULD I DO NOW?!

YOU WOULDN'T CHAIN A FRIEND TO A POST, NEITHER.

INDEED. I'VE NEVER HEARD OF A FRIEND BEING STOLEN BY BIKE THIEVES.

BUT HE **WAS** JUST A MOTORCYCLE, WASN'T HE?!

THIEVES SUCK.

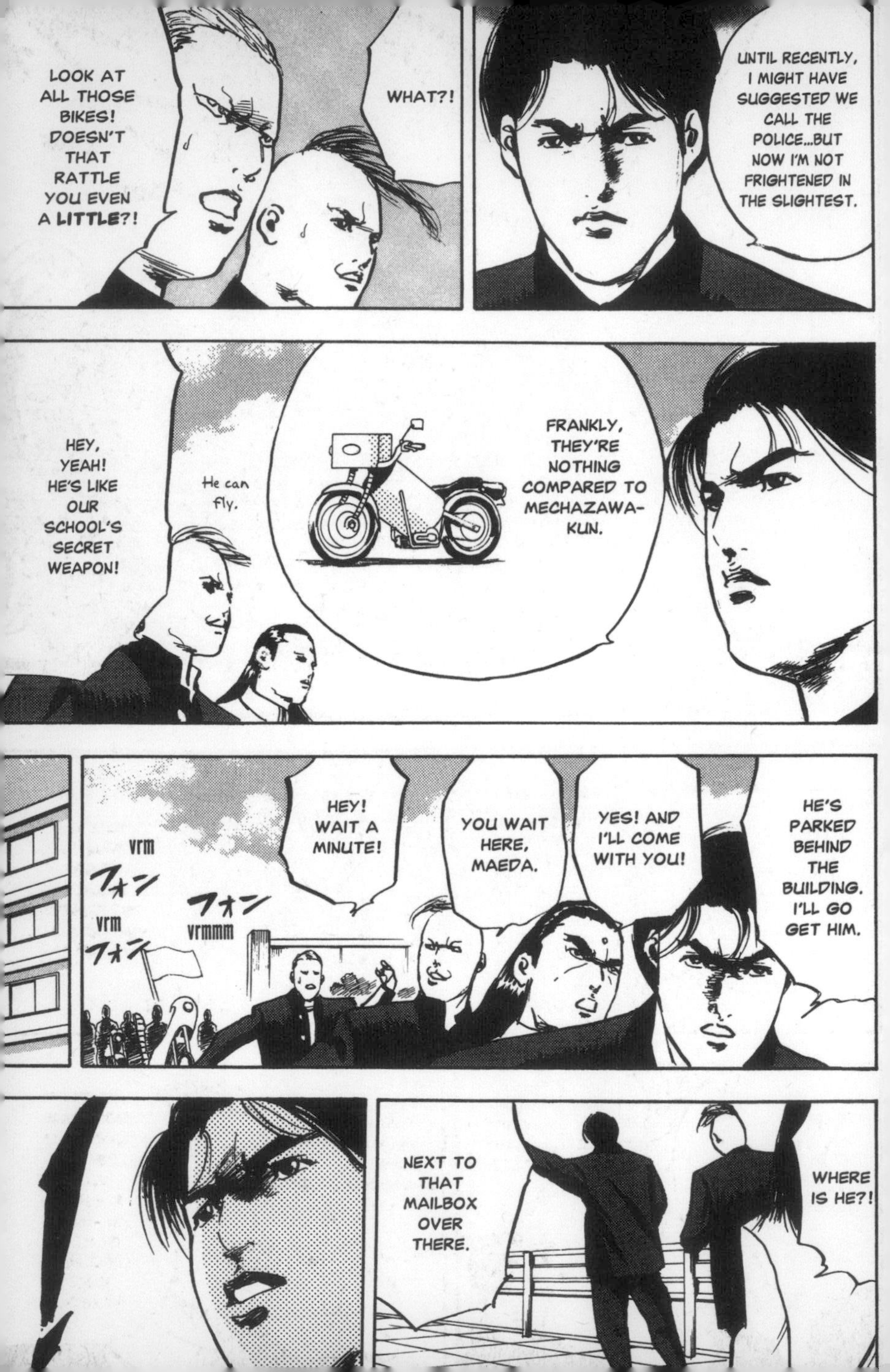
UNTIL RECENTLY, I MIGHT HAVE SUGGESTED WE CALL THE POLICE...BUT NOW I'M NOT FRIGHTENED IN THE SLIGHTEST.
WHAT?!
LOOK AT ALL THOSE BIKES! DOESN'T THAT RATTLE YOU EVEN A LITTLE?!
FRANKLY, THEY'RE NOTHING COMPARED TO MECHAZAWA-KUN.
He can fly.
HEY, YEAH! HE'S LIKE OUR SCHOOL'S SECRET WEAPON!
HE'S PARKED BEHIND THE BUILDING. I'LL GO GET HIM.
YES! AND I'LL COME WITH YOU!
YOU WAIT HERE, MAEDA.
HEY! WAIT A MINUTE!
フォン
vrmmm
vrm
フォン
vrm
フォン
WHERE IS HE?!
NEXT TO THAT MAILBOX OVER THERE.

WHOA!

フォン フォン フォン

VRRMMM
VRRMMM
VRRMMM

WE'RE GONNA BEAT YOUR ASSES TO A PULP!

rm-rm-rm-rm

THIS IS CROMARTIE, THE SO-CALLED "BADDEST HIGH SCHOOL AROUND"?!

I THINK PRACTICE IS AS GOOD AS CANCELLED!

KAMI-YAMA!

WHAT'S THE MATTER?

S-SO THEY'VE FINALLY COME TO CROMARTIE, HUH?

IT'S THAT BIKE GANG "LINEBACK"! THEY'VE BEEN RAISING ALL KINDS OF HELL AROUND HERE LATELY.

CHAPTER SIXTY-EIGHT: **TOWN CALLED MALICE**

YEAH, BUT HOKUTO'S BUNTING IS PRETTY LOUSY.

I GUESS IT IS IMPORTANT FOR THE BATTER TO BE READY FOR INSIDE PITCHES, HUH?

OK, EVERYONE! WE'VE GOT BASEBALL PRACTICE TODAY, SO LET'S GIVE IT OUR ALL!

SORRY TO BREAK IT TO YOU, BUT I THINK THAT'S JUST YOUR IMAGINATION.

YOU KNOW, IT FEELS LIKE WE'RE GETTING A LITTLE CLOSER TO KOSHIEN EVERY DAY.

WHAT?

HEY! WHAT DO YOU PUNKS THINK YOU'RE DOING?! GET OUTTA THE WAY!

VERY WELL. RIGHT IT IS!

MY RIGHT.

BY THE WAY, DO YOU SLEEP ON YOUR LEFT SIDE OR YOUR RIGHT?

UM, SIR? EXCUSE ME, BUT...

HYAAARGH!

GWAH?!

THAT'S A **BROOM** YOU'VE GOT THERE.

SO ANYTHING WILL WORK.

BUT WEREN'T THERE **GREATER** DANGERS BACK THEN? LIKE FOOD SHORTAGES AND SO FORTH?

IT'S THANKS TO HIM THAT I WAS ABLE TO SURVIVE THE WAR.

THAT CHANCE ENCOUNTER WITH THE PILLOW MASTER SAVED ME.

I CAN FINALLY SLEEP!

IT IS TRULY AN HONOR FOR US TO RECEIVE PRAISE FROM A MASTER SUCH AS YOURSELF...THOUGH PERSONALLY, I DON'T SEE WHY YOU COULDN'T JUST USE A REGULAR OLD STICK.

AFTER THAT, I TOOK UP THE CRAFT AND LEARNED THE WAY OF THE STICK FOR MYSELF. I CAN SAFELY SAY THAT YOUR COMPANY'S STICKS ARE THE BEST. THE BEST FEEL, THE BEST BALANCE, THE IDEAL WEIGHT...THESE ARE THE ONLY ONES I CAN USE ANYMORE.

M-MY FACE?

INDEED. IT'S WRITTEN ALL OVER YOUR FACE.

NO! I DIDN'T MEAN TO GIVE THAT IMPRESSION, SIR!

IT APPEARS THAT YOU DOUBT MY WORDS.

WATCH CAREFULLY.

I SHALL MAKE YOU A BELIEVER, THEN! I WILL PRESENT YOU WITH A PILLOW OF UNMATCHED QUALITY!

Y-YES, SIR.

VERY WELL. I'LL BEGIN WITH THE STORY OF MY "ENCOUNTER" WITH THE PILLOW STICK.

HUH?

YOU'RE THE ONE WHO WANTS TO HEAR ABOUT MY LIFE'S WORK?

NRGH! I'M WORRIED AND I CAN'T SLEEP!

Me when I was young

I COULD NEVER GET A GOOD NIGHT'S SLEEP. I WAS ALWAYS WORRYING ABOUT THE WAR AND WHEN IT MIGHT FINALLY END.

THE HISTORY OF THE PILLOW STICK IS QUITE OLD, DATING BACK TO THE MIDDLE OF WWII. TOKYO WAS BEING POUNDED BY AIR RAIDS, AND I WAS AMONG THOSE THAT WERE EVACUATED TO TOHOKU.

boom

b-boom

E-EXCUSE ME?

GIVE ME YOUR PILLOW, YOUNG MAN.

WHO ARE YOU?

ONE NIGHT, A MAN APPROACHED ME...

?!

IT'S SO SOFT AND FLUFFY!

UH... OK.

NOW TRY IT.

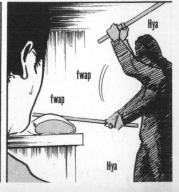

Hya

fwap

fwap

Hya

UH, YES SIR.

ONE OF OUR CLIENTS WILL BE HERE SHORTLY. GIVE THE ROOM A QUICK SWEEP, WOULD YOU?

creak

chk

SO YOU'RE THE ONE, EH?

I SEE. SO THIS COMPANY IS IN THE BUSINESS OF HITTING PILLOWS WITH STICKS.

IT IS ONLY AFTER THIS PHASE OF PRODUCTION THAT THE PILLOWS CAN BE SOLD TO CONSUMERS.

WOW! IT'S SO SOFT AND COZY!

ALSO, I THOUGHT I'D BE WORKING IN CUSTOMER SERVICE. WHAT KIND OF CUSTOMERS COULD I POSSIBLY BE SERVING?

I JUST DON'T KNOW WHAT'S WHAT ANYMORE. THIS IS A RATHER UNUSUAL COMPANY...

NO--WE **MAKE** THE STICKS! YOU DON'T CATCH ON VERY QUICKLY, DO YOU?

BUT YOU WERE USING ONE EARLIER...

CRAFTSMEN, MY BOY. IT TAKES A FAIR AMOUNT OF SKILL TO USE OUR STICKS. YOUR AVERAGE MAN ON THE STREET SIMPLY COULDN'T HANDLE SUCH A COMPLEX TOOL.

PEOPLE ACTUALLY BUY THESE? WHO?

WHY, PEOPLE BUYING OUR STICKS, OF COURSE!

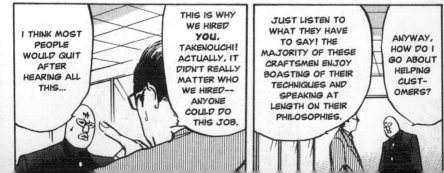

I THINK MOST PEOPLE WOULD QUIT AFTER HEARING ALL THIS...

THIS IS WHY WE HIRED **YOU**, TAKENOUCHI! ACTUALLY, IT DIDN'T REALLY MATTER WHO WE HIRED-- ANYONE COULD DO THIS JOB.

JUST LISTEN TO WHAT THEY HAVE TO SAY! THE MAJORITY OF THESE CRAFTSMEN ENJOY BOASTING OF THEIR TECHNIQUES AND SPEAKING AT LENGTH ON THEIR PHILOSOPHIES.

ANYWAY, HOW DO I GO ABOUT HELPING CUST- OMERS?

OUR PRODUCT IS RATHER...SPECIALIZED. EXPLAINING IT MAY TAKE SOME TIME, BUT LISTEN AND LISTEN WELL!

THIS IS STARTING TO FEEL LIKE A QUIZ...

NO, YOU'RE GETTING COLDER. YOUR FIRST GUESS WAS MUCH BETTER.

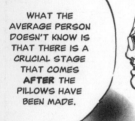

WHAT THE AVERAGE PERSON DOESN'T KNOW IS THAT THERE IS A CRUCIAL STAGE THAT COMES **AFTER** THE PILLOWS HAVE BEEN MADE.

HUH? WELL, I GUESS SO. I MEAN, I HAVEN'T REALLY THOUGHT THAT MUCH ABOUT IT.

PERHAPS YOU ARE UNDER THE IMPRESSION THAT PILLOWS MERELY COME OFF THE ASSEMBLY LINE AND ARE SOLD AS-IS.

GRIP

IT IS CALLED THE PILLOW STICK™! WE USE IT TO STRIKE PILLOWS AS THEY COME OFF THE LINE.

WHAT IS THAT?

SWP

GO AHEAD. FEEL IT.

Hya!

Hya!

fwap

fwap

FIRST, TELL ME WHAT YOU KNOW OF OUR COMPANY'S PRODUCTS.

VERY GOOD. PLEASE HAVE A SEAT.

MY NAME'S TAKENO-UCHI. I'M STARTING TODAY.

AH. BY THE WAY, WHAT SORT OF PILLOW DO YOU USE?

I'M ASHAMED TO ADMIT I APPLIED FOR THIS JOB KNOWING VERY LITTLE ABOUT YOUR COMPANY...

UH...ACTUALLY, I HAVEN'T HAD THE CHANCE TO LEARN MUCH ABOUT THEM. AT ALL.

INDEED. BAD PILLOWS CAN LEAD TO STIFF SHOULDERS. IT'S IMPORTANT TO USE **GOOD** PILLOWS, WHICH IS JUST WHAT OUR COMPANY PROVIDES.

I'VE NEVER REALLY CARED MUCH FOR PILLOWS.

PILLOW? AS IN, THE THING YOU PUT UNDER YOUR HEAD WHEN YOU GO TO SLEEP?

SO...YOU MAKE PILLOW **COVERS**?

A GOOD GUESS! BUT NOT QUITE RIGHT, I'M AFRAID.

I GET IT. YOU MANUFACTURE AND SELL PILLOWS.

CHAPTER SIXTY-SEVEN: **PILLOW TALK**

YOUR BUNTING SUCKS, HOKUTO.

WE SHOULD PRACTICE OUR COMBINATION DRILLS A LITTLE MORE TOMORROW.

MAN. ALL THIS BASEBALL IS WEARIN' ME OUT.

AH. GOOD LUCK.

WELL, I'M HEADING OUT. I START MY JOB TODAY.

YEAH, I'M GONNA RETURN THAT BOXING GLOVE. I'VE GOT A WEEK TO GET A REFUND, RIGHT?

HEY, YOU BETTER GIVE FREDDIE HIS 10,000 YEN BACK.

k-chk

CERTAINLY. IF YOU'D JUST SIGN IN.

HELLO. UM... I'M HERE TO SEE SOMEONE IN MANAGEMENT.

THEY WOULDN'T BELIEVE THAT WE'RE A BASEBALL CLUB...

THEY EVEN ARRESTED THE GORILLA.

IF YOU DON'T HAVE A BAT, YOU CAN USE A STICK. IF YOU DON'T HAVE A CATCHER'S MITT, YOU CAN USE WORK GLOVES. OR ARE YOU ALL SAYING THAT WE NEED **EXPENSIVE** EQUIPMENT TO PLAY BASEBALL?

ALL IT WILL TAKE TO OVERCOME THIS SETBACK IS FOR US TO PUT OUR HEADS TOGETHER. WHY LET IT BE THE END OF OUR FRIENDSHIP?!

WOODEN PRACTICE SWORDS! YOU KNOW, LIKE THEY USE IN KENDO! THOSE ARE NICE AND SOLID.

YEAH, BUT WHAT ARE WE GONNA USE FOR BATS?

YOU'RE RIGHT. I'LL TRY TO COME UP WITH SOME IDEAS, TOO.

WE CAN DO IT! WE CAN PLAY BALL!

NOW THAT I THINK ABOUT IT, THERE'S **LOTS** OF STUFF WE COULD USE.

WE COULD WRAP SOME CLOTH AROUND OUR WAISTS!

WHAT ABOUT CHEST PROTEC- TORS AND STUFF?

HMM. WE USE WOODEN SWORDS AND 2X4S A LOT IN FIGHTS, SO WE'RE ALREADY USED TO 'EM.

SORRY'S NOT GONNA CUT IT, IDIOT! THAT'S NOT EVEN A FRICKIN' BASEBALL GLOVE!

I'M REALLY SORRY.

I SAID I'M SORRY, AND I MEANT IT. YOU CAN KICK MY ASS IF IT'LL MAKE YOU FEEL BETTER.

WHAT THE HELL GOOD IS THAT?!

THE GUY BEHIND THE COUNTER WAS NICE, THOUGH. HE EVEN THREW IN THIS MOUTHPIECE...

grab

I'LL GIVE YOU A BEATIN' YOU'LL NEVER FORGET!

FINE!

ANYWAY, IT WAS 29,000 YEN, WHICH, YOU KNOW, AIN'T SUCH A BAD DEAL.

WELL, THERE WAS THIS TRUMPET FREDDIE REALLY HAD HIS HEART SET ON...HE WAS LIKE GLUED TO THE DISPLAY WINDOW!

THEY LEFT A ZERO OFF THE PRICE TAG...

IT WAS 290,000 YEN!

BUT WHEN THEY RANG IT UP AT THE REGISTER...

ALL WE HAVE LEFT IS 10,000 YEN.

WHY DID WE EVER TRUST THOSE TWO WITH THE MONEY?

bwaaa...

SO THIS WHOLE THING ENDED UP BEING FREDDIE GOING SHOPPING FOR HIMSELF.

YOU GOTTA LOT OF NERVE WALTZIN' BACK IN HERE AFTER PULLING A STUNT LIKE THIS!

WHAT THE HELL ARE WE GONNA DO WITH ONE GLOVE?!

ACTUALLY, UH, I USED IT. TO BUY A GLOVE.

ALRIGHT, THEN. WE'LL USE FREDDIE'S GENEROUS CONTRIBUTION TO BUY OUR EQUIPMENT.

LET'S HEAR IT FOR FREDDIE, THE WORKING MAN!

WOW, THANKS!

nod

FIVE HOURS LATER

WE'RE COUNTING ON YOU.

SEE YOU IN A BIT!

OK, HERE'S THE STORY. BUT YOU GOTTA LISTEN ALL THE WAY THROUGH, ALRIGHT?

WAIT, I DON'T UNDERSTAND. WHY DON'T YOU START FROM THE BEGINNING?

YEAH! START TALKIN'!

THEN WHAT THE HELL DID YOU SPEND IT ON?!

WE USED THE MONEY BUT WE DIDN'T BUY NO EQUIPMENT. SORRY.

UH, THERE'S SUCH A THING AS TACT.

THAT'S NO EXCUSE! IF **THIS** GUY CAN GET A JOB, THEN SO CAN YOU!

I COULD NEVER GET A JOB WITH THIS MOHAWK, SO...

I SEE. WELL, YOU CAN JUST CONTRIBUTE LATER.

I HAVE A JOB. BUT IT DOESN'T START 'TIL TOMORROW, SO I HAVEN'T EVEN GOTTEN MY FIRST PAYCHECK.

thwap

OH, YEAH. HE'S STILL WORKING AT THAT CAFÉ.

TH-THIS IS 300,000 YEN!

About $ 2,900 US

FREDDIE!

BUT...THIS IS AN AWFUL LOT OF MONEY. ARE YOU SURE ABOUT THIS, FREDDIE?

THE FINANCIAL ASSETS OF THE HOKUTO FOUNDATION ARE MORE THAN ENOUGH TO SOLVE THIS PROBLEM. NOT ONLY SHALL WE HAVE OUR OWN EQUIPMENT, WE'LL HAVE OUR OWN **STADIUM** AS WELL!

MONEY, YOU SAY? LEAVE EVERYTHING TO ME.

I'LL CALL MY DAD RIGHT NOW.

DON'T WORRY. IF THERE'S ONE WAY I CAN BE OF USE, THIS IS IT.

A-ARE YOU SURE?

MAYBE WE SHOULD JUST SCRAP THE IDEA ALTOGETHER.

For the phone.

ACTUALLY, COULD I BORROW SOME CHANGE?

WHAT DID HE SAY?

COME ON, PEOPLE! WHY DON'T WE JUST GET **JOBS**? WHERE IS YOUR SPIRIT? YOUR DETERMINATION?!

IF YOUR GOAL IS TO STOP OUR TEAM FROM EVER GETTING ONTO THE FIELD, THAT WOULD BE THE WAY TO DO IT.

I GUESS IT'S **EXTORTION** THEN.

CHAPTER SIXTY-SIX: **MONEY**

NOW THAT WE HAVE FOUNDED THE CROMARTIE BASEBALL CLUB...

WELL, THEN.

WON'T THEY LEND IT TO US?

EQUIP-MENT?

WE'LL NEED TO GET SOME EQUIPMENT.

I BELIEVE YOU'RE THINKING OF **BOWLING.**

I MEAN, I'M ALWAYS BORROW-ING THAT STUFF.

I REALIZE NOBODY WANTS TO PAY, BUT THERE'S NO WAY AROUND IT!

Pretending to be asleep

zzz

WE'LL NEED TO RAISE SOME MONEY. I'VE BEEN WEIGHING OUR OPTIONS, AND...

*On jersey: "Mom."

#4, THIRD BASE: MAEDA'S MOM.

DON'T FIGHT IT, MAEDA-KUN. AFTER ALL, THIS IS YOUR FIRST STEP TOWARD MAKING FRIENDS!

I NEVER SAID ANYTHING ABOUT WANTING TO PLAY BASEBALL!

: : :

BUT I...I'M NO ONE SPECIAL. I CAN'T DO ANYTHING.

THAT'S RIGHT. THIS CALLS FOR **UNITY**! ANYONE WHO WOULDN'T HELP OUT AT A TIME LIKE THIS CAN'T CALL HIMSELF A MAN!

And we're short-handed.

I UNDERSTAND HOW YOU FEEL. YOU'RE THINKING, "WHY ME?" THE SIMPLE TRUTH IS THAT WE NEED YOUR HELP.

NO ONE IS INFALLIBLE, MAEDA-KUN. BUT AS LONG AS YOU HAVE THE DESIRE TO PITCH IN AND HELP, I'M SURE THAT YOU'LL BE ABLE TO CONTRIBUTE TO THE TEAM.

DON'T THINK IN TERMS OF WHAT YOU "CAN" AND "CAN'T" DO. JUST CONCERN YOURSELF WITH GIVING IT YOUR ALL.

ALRIGHT. I'LL DO IT! IF THERE'S ANYTHING I CAN DO TO HELP, YOU JUST LET ME KNOW!

MORE TO THE POINT, IT'S JUST THE SAME CREW AS ALWAYS...

TWO OF 'EM AIN'T HUMAN!

HAYASHIDA? CORRECT ME IF I'M WRONG...

LET'S NOT EVEN MENTION FREDDIE ANYMORE. THERE'S NO POINT.

ALSO, UH, HIGH SCHOOL BASEBALL SHOULD BE PLAYED BY HIGH SCHOOL **STUDENTS**, RIGHT?

YOU'RE FORGETTIN' TO INCLUDE **YOURSELF**.

DON'T BE AN IDIOT, MAEDA!

BUT I'VE COUNTED YOUR MEMBERS, AND I ONLY SEE SEVEN.

YOU THINK OF EVERYTHING EXCEPT WHAT'S IMPORTANT, DON'T YOU?

NAH. I'D RATHER **LET** HIM HIT THE BALL SO I CAN CATCH IT.

OK, LET'S TALK TECHNICAL--EVEN IF YOU'RE SOME GREAT PITCHER WHO CAN STRIKE EVERYONE OUT, IF THERE'S NO ONE ELSE TO CATCH YOUR PITCHES, THE BATTER CAN JUST RUN OFF AND START STEALING BASES! DID YOU EVER THINK OF THAT?!

IT SHOULD BE NO PROBLEM. AFTER ALL, WE HAVE PLENTY OF FRIENDS.

FINE! WE'LL GET A FRICKIN' NINE-MAN TEAM!

Calm down!

LOOK, IF YOU DON'T HAVE NINE PEOPLE ON YOUR TEAM, YOU CAN'T GET APPROVED BY THE HIGH SCHOOL BASEBALL ASSOCIATION! YOU'LL NEVER GET TO THE KOSHIEN! HECK, YOU WON'T EVEN GET INTO THE REGIONALS!

I DID THE BEST I COULD, BUT I COULDN'T GET NINE PEOPLE--I COULD ONLY GET EIGHT.

I'M SORRY.

THERE'S MORE, THOUGH. I SAY I GOT EIGHT **PEOPLE**, BUT...

IT'S ONLY BEEN A DAY. BESIDES, HAVING EIGHT PEOPLE AGREE TO WORK TOGETHER AT THIS SCHOOL IS NO SMALL FEAT!

CHEER UP, HAYASHIDA-KUN.

W-WAIT A MINUTE! YOU'VE **GOT** TO HAVE NINE PEOPLE ON YOUR TEAM, PERIOD! IT'S A RULE!

DAMN, KAMIYAMA! YOU'RE ALWAYS THINKING!

YEAH...HELL, THEY'D **LIKE** FOR YOU TO HAVE LESS PLAYERS!

CONVERSELY, YOUR OPPONENT WOULD BE SURE TO PROTEST IF YOUR TEAM WAS MADE UP OF 12 PLAYERS. THEREFORE, HAVING TOO FEW PLAYERS IS BETTER THAN HAVING TOO MANY, CORRECT?

TRUE, RULES ARE A NECESSITY...BUT SOMETIMES, INNOVATION IS ACHIEVED ONLY BY **BREAKING** THE RULES. IF GALILEO HADN'T BROKEN THE RULES OF ESTABLISHED SCIENCE, WE WOULDN'T REMEMBER HIS NAME TODAY.

HUH?!

BEING BOUND BY RULES IS NO WAY TO LIVE.

YOU'RE RIGHT. I DON'T HAVE ANY FRIENDS, SO I...

YOU SHOULD WORRY ABOUT GETTIN' FRIENDS INSTEAD OF GETTIN' NINE PEOPLE ON SOME TEAM!

WHY YOU ALWAYS GOTTA BE LIKE THAT, MAEDA? JEEZ!

I'M WITH YOU, KAMI-YAMA.

HUH?!

SIMILARLY, IF PEOPLE ARE BOUND BY RULES, THEY'LL NEVER BE ABLE TO MOVE FORWARD. THAT'S WHY YOU'RE UNABLE TO MAKE FRIENDS.

RELAX, MAEDA. I CAN HIT HOMERUNS **AND** CATCH BALLS, SO THERE'S NO PROBLEM.

BASEBALL IS PLAYED BY TEAMS OF NINE! YOU CAN'T HAVE A ONE-PERSON TEAM!

HEY! THAT'S NOT THE ISSUE HERE.

FAR BE IT FROM ME TO RUIN THE MOMENT, BUT THERE'S SOMETHING I WANT TO ASK YOU, HAYASHIDA--DO YOU EVEN KNOW **HOW** TO PLAY BASEBALL? LIKE, THE RULES?

WHAT THE HECK DO **YOU** WANT?!

WAIT A MINUTE!

THAT'S NOT A RULE!

FIRST, YOU GOTTA SHAVE YOUR HEAD.

OF COURSE I DO!

NO, YOU CAN'T! IT'S AGAINST THE RULES!

NOT TO WORRY. I CAN DO JUST FINE ON MY OWN!

ANYWAY, YOU NEED **NINE** PEOPLE TO START A TEAM! DID YOU EVEN KNOW THAT?!

BUT I DOUBT YOU'D HEAR ANY COMPLAINTS IF YOUR TEAM HAD, SAY, **FIVE** PEOPLE, AFTER ALL, IT WOULD BE TO YOUR OPPONENT'S ADVANTAGE.

I'LL CONCEDE TO YOU ON THIS "NINE PERSON RULE" MATTER...

YOU DON'T KNOW HOW TO PLAY EITHER, DO YOU?

I'M INCLINED TO DISAGREE WITH YOU AS WELL, MAEDA-KUN.

DON'T WORRY.

KAMIYAMA...

IN BASEBALL, THE MOST IMPORTANT THING ISN'T SKILL--IT'S THE DESIRE TO PLAY THE GAME! SO LONG AS YOU HAVE THE **PASSION**, THAT'S ALL THAT COUNTS.

whoa

ANY TIME. I'M GLAD TO BE OF SERVICE.

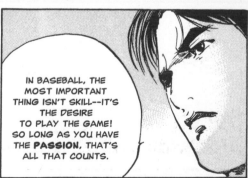

THAT WAS JUST WHAT I NEEDED TO HEAR! THANKS, MAN!

CHAPTER SIXTY-FIVE: **WITHOUT YOU**

I WANNA GO TO THE KOSHIEN BASEBALL CHAMPIONSHIP!

YOU'RE KIND OF, UH, EASILY INFLUENCED, AREN'T YOU?

I'VE WANTED TO SINCE I SAW IT ON TV LAST SUMMER.

YOU JUST QUIT? HOW ARE YOU EVER GONNA PLAY BALL WITH THAT KIND OF ATTITUDE?! YOU MIGHT AS WELL GIVE UP NOW!

I QUIT. AND SEEING AS HOW I WAS THE ONLY MEMBER, THERE'S NO MORE CLUB.

HEY, ME AND THE OTHER BADASSES WAS TALKIN'-- WEREN'T YOU IN THE **BOXING CLUB** OR SOMETHIN'? WHAT HAPPENED WITH THAT?

SWP

YOU'RE PROBABLY RIGHT. I GUESS I'M JUST NOT CUT OUT FOR KOSHIEN...

STUDENT PROFILE   DATE (MM/DD/YY)

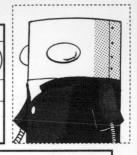

NAME	M	F
Shinichi Mechazawa		

DATE OF BIRTH (MM/DD/YY)   1/1/   (AGE   )

ADDRESS

Sipin-ku, Thomason 1-4-3. Tokyo.

YEAR	MONTH	ACADEMICS/WORK EXPERIENCE
	Mar	Sipin-ku, Thomason Elementary. Graduated.
	Mar	Sipin-ku, Thomason Middle School. Graduated.
	Apr	Tokyo, Cromartie High School. Enrolled.

YEAR	MONTH	CERTIFICATIONS/OTHER
		I'm no good with bikes or other machines, so I don't
		have any licenses.

ACADEMIC STRENGTHS

Art, modern Japanese

PERSONAL STRENGTHS AND WEAKNESSES

Strength: Very manly
Weakness: Terrible with machines

PEOPLE YOU ADMIRE

Ken Takakura, Koji Tsuruta

SPECIAL SKILLS

-Fighting
-Body is extraordinarily hard

GOALS

I'm just a boring guy with no particularly noteworthy
characteristics, but I look forward to attending school here.

INSTRUCTIONS

1. Please use blue or black ink only.   2. Please write neatly.

STUDENT PROFILE   DATE (MM/DD/YY)

NAME		M F
→ Freddie		

DATE OF BIRTH (MM/DD/YY)   / /   (AGE   )

ADDRESS

YEAR	MONTH	ACADEMICS/WORK EXPERIENCE

YEAR	MONTH	CERTIFICATIONS/OTHER

ACADEMIC STRENGTHS	PERSONAL STRENGTH AND WEAKNESSES

PEOPLE YOU ADMIRE	SPECIAL SKILLS

GOALS

I wrote this (Hayashida)

INSTRUCTIONS

1. Please use blue or black ink only.   2. Please write neatly.

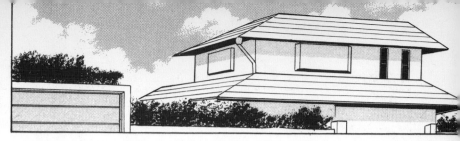

I FORGOT TO TAKE THE MASK OFF!

I-I GOT THE JOB?!

IT'S THE MAN WHO INTERVIEWED YOU. HE SAYS YOU'RE HIRED.

TRY TO BE MORE CAREFUL IN THE SHOWER.

UM...WELL, THE MOST IMPORTANT PART OF CUSTOMER SERVICE IS TO SIMPLY ENJOY WORKING WITH PEOPLE, WHICH IS SOMETHING YOU'VE TOUCHED ON ALREADY. IN THAT ASPECT, YOU SEEM VERY WELL-SUITED FOR THE TYPE OF WORK WE DO.

TH-THANK YOU VERY MUCH, SIR!

HE CERTAINLY DOESN'T!

IN MORE WAYS THAN ONE...

YOUR ANSWER WAS ALSO REMARKABLY WELL THOUGHT OUT. YOU HARDLY SEEM LIKE A HIGH SCHOOL STUDENT AT ALL!

YES, SIR! THANK YOU, SIR!

WELL, THAT ABOUT WRAPS THINGS UP. WE'LL CONTACT YOU ONCE WE'VE MADE OUR DECISION.

STILL, I GUESS I'LL TRY TO LINE UP SOME OTHER INTERVIEWS, TOO. JUST TO BE SAFE.

I THINK MY ANSWER SHOWED THEM I'VE GOT THE DRIVE AND AMBITION THEY'RE AFTER.

SO...YOU'RE A HIGH SCHOOL STUDENT?

YES, SIR! I'LL BE 16 YEARS OLD THIS SEPTEMBER!

I SEE. THERE ARE A FEW QUESTIONS I'D LIKE TO ASK YOU...

FIRST, WHY DO YOU WANT TO WORK FOR THIS COMPANY?

YOUR COMPANY HAS STORES ALL OVER JAPAN, AND IF YOU DON'T MIND ME SAYING SO, I THOUGHT THAT I WOULD BE A GOOD MATCH FOR THE KIND OF WORK YOU DO. SO I DECIDED TO APPLY FOR THIS POSITION.

SIR! BASICALLY I ENJOY WORKING WITH PEOPLE, AND HAVE BEEN INTERESTED IN CUSTOMER SERVICE FOR SOME TIME NOW.

CHAPTER SIXTY-FOUR: **INTERVIEW WITH THE MASKED MAN**

shhh

pssssh

MASKED TAKENOUCHI: A HIJACKER BEING HUNTED BY THE LAW. TO EVADE AUTHORITIES HE IS MASQUERADING AS TAKENOUCHI. NOBODY HAS NOTICED.

WHERE ARE YOU OFF TO SO EARLY? THERE'S NO SCHOOL TODAY.

HEY, MOM! COULD YOU HAND ME A TOWEL?

chk

I'VE BEEN KINDA LOW ON FUNDS LATELY, SO I'VE BEEN LOOKING AROUND FOR WORK. BESIDES, IT'LL BE A GOOD EXPERIENCE.

rub

rub

I'VE GOT A JOB INTERVIEW.

AHEM

JOB INTERVIEWS HELD HERE

WHAT DO I DO NOW? THE GUYS WILL BE PISSED AT ME!

UUNNGH ≋SNIFFLE≋

WHOOPS! I GUESS TAKING ON A SCHOOL ALL ALONE IS BITING OFF MORE THAN YOU CAN CHEW! POOR KUWAHARA-KUN.

RRNGH

HUH?

IT'S OK.

I'M SORRY...I'M SO SORRY! ≋SOB≋ I LOST THE FIGHT! UUNNNGH...

IMAMURA-SAN!

KUWA-HARA!

GOOD FOR YOU, KUWAHARA-KUN. YOU DID SWELL!

THANK YOU! THANKS SO MUCH!

AND YOU FOUGHT LIKE THE BEST OF 'EM. TODAY YOU'RE ONE STEP CLOSER TO BEING A MAN.

IT DOESN'T MATTER IF YOU WIN OR LOSE. THE IMPORTANT THING IS THAT YOU HAD THE **COURAGE** TO FIGHT.

IT IS?

TH-THAT'S A GREAT STORY.

HIS FIRST ERRAND
The Story of a Badass

The End

THEY'RE AT MAEDA'S HOUSE.

A-HA! KUWAHARA-KUN, BADASS THAT HE IS, DECIDED TO IGNORE THE ATTENDANT AND RIDE THE TRAIN WITHOUT PAYING. GOOD THINKING!

SIR! YOUR TICKET!

AH, WHO CARES?

OH, NO! HE MUST HAVE DROPPED IT DURING THAT FIGHT EARLIER!

CRAP! I LOST MY MONEY!

DAMN! I MISSED MY STOP!

BUT NOW HE'S FALLEN ASLEEP!

vwoosh

LET'S NOT BE HASTY, KUWAHARA-KUN!

I GUESS IT DOESN'T MATTER **WHERE** I GO SO LONG AS I PICK A FIGHT ONCE I'M THERE!

OR ELSE THE OTHERS WILL GET MAD AT ME.

HE FORGOT THE MOST IMPORTANT PART! OH, THE SUSPENSE!

UH... WHERE WAS I GOIN' ANYWAY?

OK, THIS PLACE LOOKS GOOD.

HMPH!

(CUE NARRATION)

AND JUST LIKE THAT, KUWAHARA-KUN WAS ON HIS WAY TO HIS VERY FIRST "SCHOOL RAID." BUT WITH SO MANY BADASSES LYING IN WAIT, WHAT WILL BECOME OF HIM?

OH, DEAR. THAT'S A PRETTY DANGEROUS-LOOKING TRIO COMING HIS WAY. WILL KUWAHARA BE ABLE TO BEAT DOWN ALL THREE OF THEM?

LOOKS LIKE THREE AGAINST ONE WAS A LITTLE TOO MUCH FOR OUR KUWAHARA.

COULD A FIGHT BE BREWING?

WHAT?!

SCREW YOU, APE!

HUH?!

wobble

BUT HE STILL MANAGES TO PICK HIMSELF UP AND WALK TO THE STATION. WHAT A TROOPER!

CHAPTER SIXTY-THREE: **WALK THIS WAY**

HUH? ME?!

BUT THERE'S NO NEED FOR ME TO DEAL WITH A BUNCH OF PUNKS LIKE THEM PERSONALLY. SO I'M LEAVING IT TO YOU, KUWAHARA.

THOSE IDIOTS AT BOOMER HIGH HAVE BEEN GETTIN' PRETTY COCKY LATELY. IT'S TIME TO GO TEACH 'EM A LESSON.

YEAH! AND IF YOU KEEP TALKIN' CRAP LIKE THAT, YOU'LL NEVER AMOUNT TO NOTHIN'!

THEN THIS IS A GOOD PLACE TO START. NOW GET GOIN'!

B-BUT I'M JUST A 1ST YEAR! I DON'T REALLY KNOW MUCH ABOUT, UH, HOW THIS WHOLE BADASS THING WORKS YET!

HIS FIRST ERRAND

THE STORY OF A BADASS

GOOD! NOW GO AND GET THE JOB DONE **RIGHT!**

VERY WELL. I'LL BE LEAVING THEN, SIR.

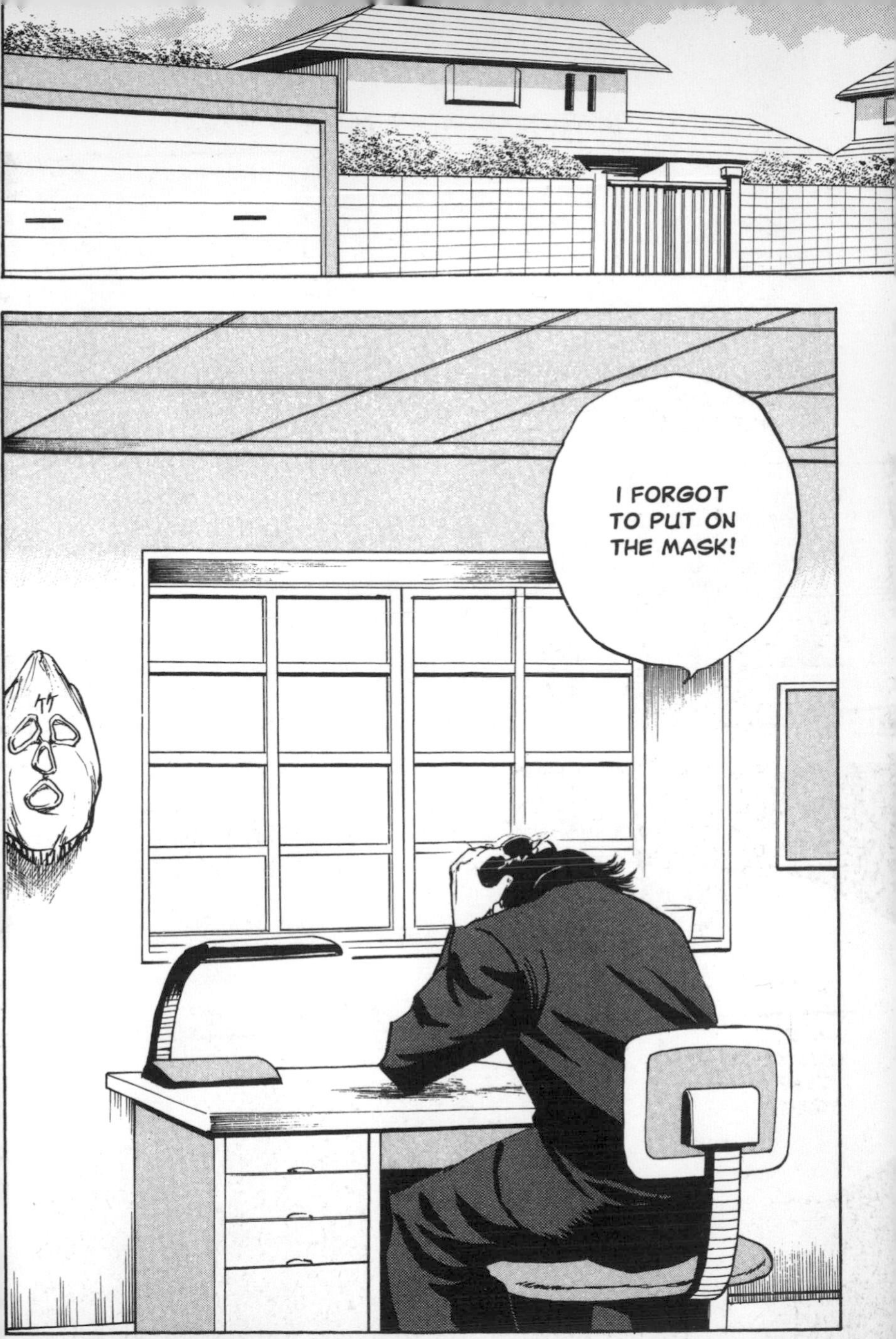
I FORGOT TO PUT ON THE MASK!

MASKED TAKENOUCHI!

AND ME. I KEPT WANTING TO SAY IT, BUT I COULDN'T FIND THE RIGHT TIME.

NO WAY! I'VE GOT SOMETHING, TOO!

HUH? YEAH, ME TOO!

IS HE A TRANSFER STUDENT OR SOMETHING?

DUNNO. I NEVER SAW HIM BEFORE.

WHO WAS THAT GUY?!

!!

OR DON'T YOU EVER WONDER WHY YOU WERE BORN?

SLAM

HE MADE US REALIZE WHAT WE'D FORGOTTEN. THAT GUY'S SOMETHIN' ELSE.

YEAH! IT'S LIKE, THE HIGHER PEOPLE CLIMB, THE MORE PROTECTIVE AND STUFF THEY GET!

HE'S RIGHT! WE FORGOT WHAT BEING *BAD* IS ALL ABOUT!

BUT THERE'S SOMETHING I'VE BEEN WONDERING...

HE'S PRETTY AMAZING, ALRIGHT.

WHAT DO YOU THINK YOU'RE DOING?!

GWAGH!

whump

CH-CHANGED? WHAT ARE YOU TALKIN' ABOUT?!

FROM TODAY ON, I'M A CHANGED MAN.

YOU GUYS ARE LOOKING AT THE NEW ME.

IT'S EASY TO TALK TOUGH, BUT EVERYONE VALUES THEIR LIVES, YOU KNOW!

...

THE OLD ME WAS A COWARD. I WAS ALWAYS LOOKIN' FOR A WAY OUT, TRYIN' TO THINK OF WAYS TO AVOID CONFLICT.... JUST LIKE YOU ARE NOW.

...

BUT WHAT'S THE FUN OF SPENDING THAT WHOLE TIME PLAYIN' IT SAFE?

AT MOST, PEOPLE LIVE FOR LIKE 100 YEARS.

WE'LL BE OUT-NUMBERED!

YEAH, I'M POSITIVE.

YOU SURE ABOUT THAT?

I HEARD BASS AND DESTRADE ARE PLANNIN' TO TEAM UP. THEY'RE GONNA GET A GANG TOGETHER AND COME AFTER US!

INSTEAD OF WASTING TIME WORRYIN' ABOUT WHAT THEY'RE GONNA DO, WHY NOT JUST GO TAKE 'EM ALL OUT?

HUH?!

GO KILL 'EM, THEN.

WHOA, HOLD ON! IF THOSE GUYS GANG UP, IT DOESN'T MATTER HOW STRONG WE...

CRACK

YEAH! BRING IT OR ELSE!

YOU BETTER HAVE SOME MONEY LATER THIS WEEK!

IT'S EASY TO JUST ROLL OVER ON YOUR STOMACH WHEN SOMEBODY POWERFUL COMES ALONG. HELL, YOU'LL EVEN LIVE LONGER THAT WAY.

THANKS. I...I OWE YOU.

BUT YOU KNOW WHAT? THAT AIN'T LIVIN'--THAT'S SOMEBODY **LETTIN'** YOU LIVE. AND YOU'LL HAVE THAT HANGIN' 'ROUND YOUR NECK 'TIL THE DAY YOU DIE.

RGH!

crKk

OW...

fwap

LET GO, DAMN IT!

YOU HEARD THAT NOZOKI-KUN WAS IN A BIKE ACCIDENT, RIGHT? WELL, WE STARTED TAKIN' DONATIONS FOR HIM. HOW ABOUT HANDIN' OVER A LITTLE CASH?

YOU 1ST YEARS SURE AIN'T BEEN GIVIN' US MUCH RESPECT LATELY! YOU'RE ASKIN' FOR IT, YOU KNOW THAT?!

WHAT?!

UH, SORRY. I REALLY DON'T HAVE ANYTHING ON ME.

AND DON'T COME BACK WITHOUT YOUR WALLET!

NOW GO HOME AND GET SOME MONEY!

GRAB

WHO THE HELL ARE YOU?!

NAME ☑M ☐F

Masked Takenouchi

DATE OF BIRTH (MM/DD/YY)   *7/7/*   (AGE   )

ADDRESS

Takenouchi's house

YEAR	MONTH	ACADEMICS/WORK EXPERIENCE
		It's all secret.
		Though, I can tell you that I've spent time in a Mexican prison.

YEAR	MONTH	CERTIFICATIONS/OTHER
		Have all sorts of licenses
		Certified master of Pillow-jutsu

ACADEMIC STRENGTHS

Spanish

PERSONAL STRENGTHS AND WEAKNESSES

Strength - Poker face.
Weaknesses - Sometimes forget to put my mask on. Also, I tend to get nervous when it comes to "the big fight."

PEOPLE YOU ADMIRE

Mil Máscaras

SPECIAL SKILLS

-Can make pillows soft.

-Soon make friends with others.

GOALS
To hurry up and take this mask off!

STUDENT PROFILE   **DATE (MM/DD/YY)**

NAME	M / F
Noboru Yamaguchi	出

DATE OF BIRTH (MM/DD/YY)	11/23	(AGE)

ADDRESS

Destrade-ku, Burkleo Street 1-9. Tokyo.

YEAR	MONTH	ACADEMICS/WORK EXPERIENCE
	Mar	Destrade-ku, Terry Elementary. Graduated.
	Mar	Destrade-ku, Steve Middle School. Graduated.
	Apr	Tokyo, Destrade Industrial High School. Enrolled.

YEAR	MONTH	CERTIFICATIONS/OTHER
		Motorcycle License

ACADEMIC STRENGTHS

Operating a lathe, Arc welding

PERSONAL STRENGTHS AND WEAKNESSES

Strength - Can identify comic potential faster than anyone else.

Weakness- Haven't had much luck getting laughs recently.

PEOPLE YOU ADMIRE

Buster Keaton
Ohyoi and Tamori
The comic duo "Summer's" (the guy without glasses)

SPECIAL SKILLS

-Write jokes for local radio shows.
-Making people laugh (though I haven't actually tried yet).

GOALS

I want to hurry up and make my debut so I can restore the comic industry to normal.

INSTRUCTIONS

1. Please use blue or black ink only.   2. Please write neatly.

THIS KINDA THING HAPPENS A LOT WITH NEWBIES. HE DOESN'T SEEM LIKE SUCH A BAD GUY, THOUGH. I GUESS I SHOULD REPLY...

HE APOLO-GIZED!

I'M REALLY SORRY FOR CAUSING TROUBLE. I JUST STARTED USING THE INTERNET, SO I'VE GOT A LOT TO LEARN. I THOUGHT ABOUT WHAT YOU SAID, AND I REALIZE NOW THAT I WAS WRONG. THANKS FOR BEING SO PATIENT. I'LL TRY TO BE MORE POLITE.

MM?!

OH YEAH? LET'S GO PAY HIM A VISIT.

FUJIMOTO-SAN? THAT NEW GUY JUST CALLED. HE SAYS HE WANTS TO APOLOGIZE FOR HOW HE'S BEEN ACTIN'. I GUESS HE'S NOT SUCH A BAD GUY AFTER ALL.

"PLEASE, THINK NOTHING OF IT! :) WE ALL HAVE TO START SOMEWHERE. ACTUALLY, I WAS BEING A LITTLE CHILDISH MYSELF... ANYWAY, HERE'S MY EMAIL ADDRESS IN CASE YOU EVER HAVE QUESTIONS ABOUT ANYTHING. SEE YOU!" DONE.

click
click
click

I JUST DON'T GET THIS GUY...

IT'S A LITTLE LATE FOR APOLOGIES, ASSHOLE!

BWOCK

THEY CALL HIM THE ONLINE KINGPIN ^_^

HUH?!

FORGET IT. JUST LET IT GO.

I GUESS WE WENT TOO EASY ON HIM. WE GOTTA SHOW HIM WHO'S BOSS! GET THAT GUY IN HERE!

THAT NEW GUY'S BEEN TALKING ABOUT YOU BEHIND YOUR BACK. HE'S BEEN SAYIN' ALL KINDS OF CRAP!

UH...

WHAT A WASTE OF TIME. I'M OUTTA HERE!

IT JUST GOES TO SHOW WHAT A **CHUMP** HE REALLY IS. BESIDES, I CAN'T GO BEATIN' THE HELL OUT OF EVERY GUY WHO TALKS SMACK ABOUT ME.

IF HE'S GOT SOMETHIN' TO SAY, LET HIM SAY IT. WHO CARES IF HE'S TALKIN' ABOUT ME BEHIND MY BACK?

THAT LAST REPLY I WROTE WAS TOO MUCH.

IS THIS WHAT IT'S LIKE TO BE IN LOVE WITH ANOTHER MAN?!

MAN, THAT GUY'S ON A WHOLE DIFFERENT LEVEL.

chk

PLEASE, DON'T LET THEM SAY ANYTHING BAD ABOUT ME...

THAT KINDA STUFF JUST MAKES ME SO NERVOUS! AARGH!

WHAT'LL I DO IF PEOPLE START WRITING BAD THINGS ABOUT ME, OR **FLAMING** ME?!

WHAT...

HEY, SOMEONE REPLIED ALREADY.

HUH?

JEEZ, WHAT A BUNCH OF WIMPS. YOU GOTTA BE TOUGH, OR YOU'RE **FINISHED!**

IT'S THAT SONOFABITCH AGAIN! AND HE'S MOCKING **ME!** DOESN'T HE KNOW WHO I AM?! THAT'S IT--I'M GONNA HAVE TO SET THIS GUY STRAIGHT!

NRRGH!

USERNAME: UNREGISTERED USER

ISN'T IT AGAINST THE RULES TO POST OFF-TOPIC COMMENTS? STILL, IF YOU'RE JUST A TROLL WITH NOTHING BETTER TO DO THAN CAUSE TROUBLE, I GUESS THIS WARNING WON'T MAKE MUCH OF A DIFFERENCE. OH, WHAT A BOTHER! (LOL)

"I HAVE BEEN (IF YOU DON'T MIND ME POINTING OUT) AN ACTIVE MEMBER OF THIS BOARD FOR TWO YEARS, LONG BEFORE YOU POSTED HERE. WHILE THIS DOES NOT NECESSARILY MEAN I AM YOUR 'SUPERIOR,' I CAN SAY WITH SOME AUTHORITY THAT YOU HAVE YET TO GRASP THE BASIC RULES OF ONLINE ETIQUETTE. IF YOU DISAGREE WITH ANYTHING I HAVE SAID HERE, FEEL FREE TO POST A RESPONSE. APOLOGIES IN ADVANCE FOR ANY HURT FEELINGS." THERE!

click
click
click

"WHILE IT IS INDEED AGAINST BOARD POLICY TO POST OFF-TOPIC COMMENTS, WE RISK DOING MORE HARM THAN GOOD IF WE LIMIT OURSELVES TO A STRICT INTERPRETATION OF THIS LAW."

"PROVIDED NOBODY MINDS, THERE IS SOMETHING I WOULD LIKE TO SAY IN RESPONSE."

click

HEAR WHAT?

HEY, FUJI-MOTO. DID YOU HEAR?

MANUEL HIGH

I GUESS I WAS A LITTLE HARD ON THE GUY, BUT I HAD NO CHOICE. YOU CAN'T TALK FACE-TO-FACE ONLINE, SO THERE CAN BE ALL KINDS OF MISUNDERSTANDINGS IF YOU DON'T MAKE YOURSELF CLEAR.

"NOT TO CHANGE THE SUBJECT, BUT I'VE NOTICED THAT MORE AND MORE PEOPLE ARE TALKING ABOUT BROADBAND. I'M STILL USING ISDN AT HOME, AND IT SEEMS TO BE RUNNING PRETTY SLOW THESE DAYS. I'M STARTING TO THINK ABOUT SWITCHING TO DSL."

click
click
click

"WITH SO MANY PEOPLE VISITING THE SITE LATELY, THINGS SURE HAVE GOTTEN LIVELY AROUND HERE, HAVEN'T THEY? I FOR ONE AM GLAD TO SEE ALL THIS NEW ACTIVITY."

OH, THAT'S RIGHT-- I SHOULD SEND THE ADMIN A CARD OR SOMETHING. IT'S ABOUT TIME I TRIED DRAWING SOME CG PICS OF MY OWN, ANYWAY.

"I KNOW THIS DOESN'T HAVE ANYTHING TO DO WITH POOTAN, BUT IT'S OK TO GET OFF-TOPIC EVERY ONCE IN A WHILE, RIGHT? ANYWAY, SORRY. ^_^;; "

click
click

WELL, WE THINK YOU MIGHT BE GOING A LITTLE HARD ON THE NEW GUYS. I MEAN, NONE OF **US** KNEW HOW THINGS WORKED WHEN WE WERE NEW. SO, MAYBE YOU COULD TRY, LIKE...EXPLAINING THINGS TO 'EM FIRST, IF YOU DON'T MIND.

YEAH?

UH, BOSS? ME AND THE OTHER GUYS WERE TALKIN' YESTERDAY ...

UH, RIGHT...

IF THEY STILL DON'T GET IT, I COULD ALWAYS BREAK A COUPLE FINGERS.

IF I NEED TO EXPLAIN SOMETHIN', I'LL DO IT WITH MY **FISTS**.

FORGET IT. I HATE THAT KINDA STUFF.

OH. UH, OK.

IS THAT RIGHT? I BETTER GO SEE HIM, THEN.

WELL...WE JUST GOT THIS NEW MEMBER IN OUR GANG, AND THE GUY'S GOT KIND OF AN ATTITUDE. HE SAYS HE WANTS TO TALK WITH YOU **DIRECTLY.**

THAT'S FUJIMOTO FOR YA. HE DOESN'T GO EASY ON ANYONE, EVEN THE NEW GUYS!

H-HE BROKE HIS NOSE!

YOU GOT A LOTTA NERVE, BOY!

BWACK

AND HE'S SO NICE TO THEM ONLINE...

"SAY, I HAVEN'T SEEN AYUMARO-SAN HERE IN A WHILE. KNOWING HIM, HE'S PROBABLY BUSY WITH WORK. LOL." HUH?

click

click

click

"HELLO AGAIN, EVERYONE! HOW ARE YOU ALL DOING? IT CERTAINLY HAS BEEN HOT LATELY, HASN'T IT?"

UNBELIEVABLE! WE WERE ALL HAVING A GOOD TIME, AND THEN THIS GUY HAD TO COME ALONG AND SAY SOMETHING RUDE!

HEY! WHAT KIND OF POST IS THIS?

WHAT THE...

POOTAN'S WEB PAGE
Forums

USERNAME: UNREGISTERED USER
DATE: 6/20/2001

POOTAN SUCKS! EVERYONE ON THIS FORUM IS AN IDIOT!!!1

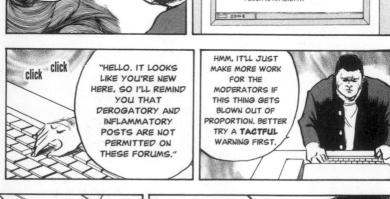

click   click

"HELLO. IT LOOKS LIKE YOU'RE NEW HERE, SO I'LL REMIND YOU THAT DEROGATORY AND INFLAMMATORY POSTS ARE NOT PERMITTED ON THESE FORUMS."

HMM, IT'LL JUST MAKE MORE WORK FOR THE MODERATORS IF THIS THING GETS BLOWN OUT OF PROPORTION. BETTER TRY A **TACTFUL** WARNING FIRST.

HUH?

PHONE'S FOR YOU.

"AND EVEN THOUGH THIS IS YOUR FIRST POST, I WOULD RECOMMEND YOU REGISTER A USERNAME. OTHERWISE, FUTURE POSTS WILL BE SEEN AS IRRESPONSIBLE AND NOT TO BE TAKEN SERIOUSLY. PLEASE TRY TO ABIDE BY THE FORUM RULES. THANK YOU." THERE, THAT SHOULD DO.

click

click

JUST STANDING NEXT TO THE GUY SENDS SHIVERS DOWN MY SPINE.

THAT FUJIMOTO FREAKS ME OUT. HE'S LIKE A DEMON!

GOOD. I'M GOIN' HOME. YOU TAKE CARE OF THE REST.

FUJI-MOTO'S

LET'S SEE HERE...

KIICHI FUJIMOTO
MANUEL HIGH SCHOOL

BWOMP

CRACK

THAT'S **ONE** DOWN.

bwack

bwack

Y-YES, SIR!

THERE AIN'T NO RULES IN A FIGHT. GOT IT?!

YOU GOTTA BEAT 'EM UNTIL THEY STOP MOVIN'.

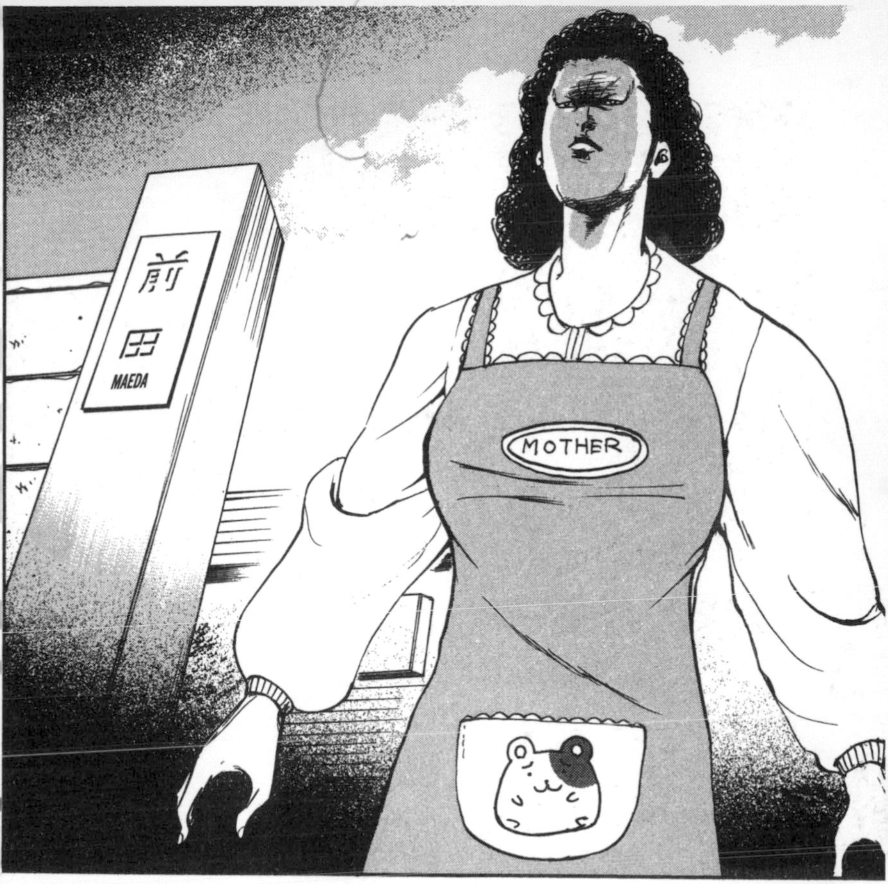
前田
MAEDA
MOTHER

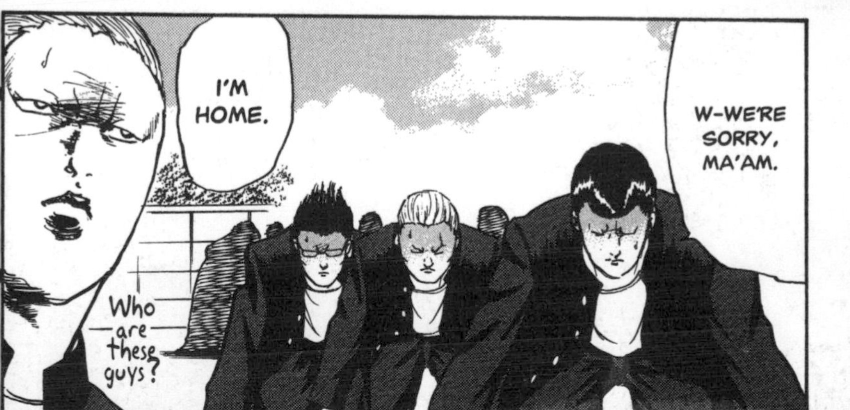
W-WE'RE SORRY, MA'AM.
I'M HOME.
Who are these guys?

THE APRON'S A NICE TOUCH.

WHAT?!

HOW ABOUT IT, ITO? MIND IF WE GO OVER TO YOUR HOUSE AND MEET YOUR DAD?

HEY, I'M A LOT HIGHER PROFILE THAN YOU, BUT I SWALLOWED MY PRIDE AND SHOWED YOU THAT PICTURE. I DON'T MIND TELLING YOU I'M PRETTY DAMN EMBARRASSED RIGHT NOW...BUT THE POINT I'M GETTING AT IS, COULD **YOU** ALL DO THE SAME?

Y-YOU'RE GOIN' TOO FAR, MAN!

ANY-THING BUT THAT!

C'MON, MAN!

NO PROBLEM. WE'RE ONLY GOING TO SEE WHAT YOUR DAD LOOKS LIKE.

NO! I-I MEAN, THE PLACE IS A MESS! IT AIN'T CLEAN!

NOW DO YOU UNDERSTAND? THAT'S HOW AFRAID HE IS OF LETTING US SEE HIS FATHER.

"MAD DOG" ITO IS ON HIS HANDS AND KNEES! I DON'T BELIEVE IT!

DUDE, HE'S PROS-TRATIN' HIMSELF!

bwsh

PLEASE!

LET'S SEE WHAT HIS FOLKS LOOK LIKE!

OK, THIS IS WHERE ONE OF THOSE CROMARTIE GUYS LIVES.

CROMARTIE DOESN'T STAND A CHANCE!

THE MOST EMBARRASSING THING...HEY, DO BADASSES EVEN **GET** EMBARRASSED?!

WE NEED TO FIGURE OUT THE MOST EMBARRASSING THING THAT COULD HAPPEN TO A BADASS.

YEAH! WE GOTTA FIND SOME WAY TO EMBARRASS THE HELL OUT OF THEM!

HUH?

TAKE A LOOK AT THIS PICTURE.

HUH?!

MY DAD.

WHO IS THIS LOSER ANYWAY?

HE LOOKS LIKE ONE OF THEM "BUSINESS-MEN."

I DON'T GET IT. IT'S JUST SOME OLD DUDE.

JUST IMAGINE PHOTOS OF YOUR PARENTS BEING PASSED AROUND TO OTHERS. IT WOULD BE THE DEATH OF YOUR REPUTATION AS A BADASS! LIKE FINDING OUT THAT ONE OF THOSE "BAD GUY" WRESTLERS HAD A KID AND WAS ACTUALLY A DOTING PARENT...

BY THE WAY, I CALL THAT DUDE "FATHER" WHEN I'M AT HOME.

IT DOESN'T MATTER HOW BAD YOU MIGHT LOOK--YOUR **PARENTS** ARE ALWAYS GONNA LOOK NORMAL.

CHAPTER FIFTY-NINE: **NOTHIN' TO LOSE**

WE WENT ALL THAT WAY FOR NOTHIN'!

IT'S HOPELESS, MAN, HOPELESS!

WHO WOULD'VE THOUGHT THEY WOULDN'T BE WEARIN' ANY PANTS?!

DAMMIT! WHAT DO WE DO NOW?

BASS HIGH STRATEGY MEETING

VERY WELL. THIS ROUND GOES TO CROMARTIE.

YOU'VE GOT TO HAND IT TO THEM--THEY CERTAINLY HAVE A **DIFFERENT** WAY OF DOING THINGS.

OF COURSE! THE BELL FOR ROUND TWO HAS ALREADY RUNG.

YOU MEAN YOU WANT TO GO UP AGAINST 'EM AGAIN?!

"THIS ROUND"?

THAT BEING SAID, WHY SHOULD WE HAVE TO LIMIT OURSELVES TO THEIR PANTS?! IF WE WANT TO CRUSH CROMARTIE ONCE AND FOR ALL, WHAT WE NEED TO STEAL IS THEIR **PRIDE**!

I WOULDN'T BE SO SURE. I THINK THIS GUY WAS JUST AN ISOLATED CASE.

BUT THEY DON'T HAVE ANY PANTS FOR US TO TAKE!

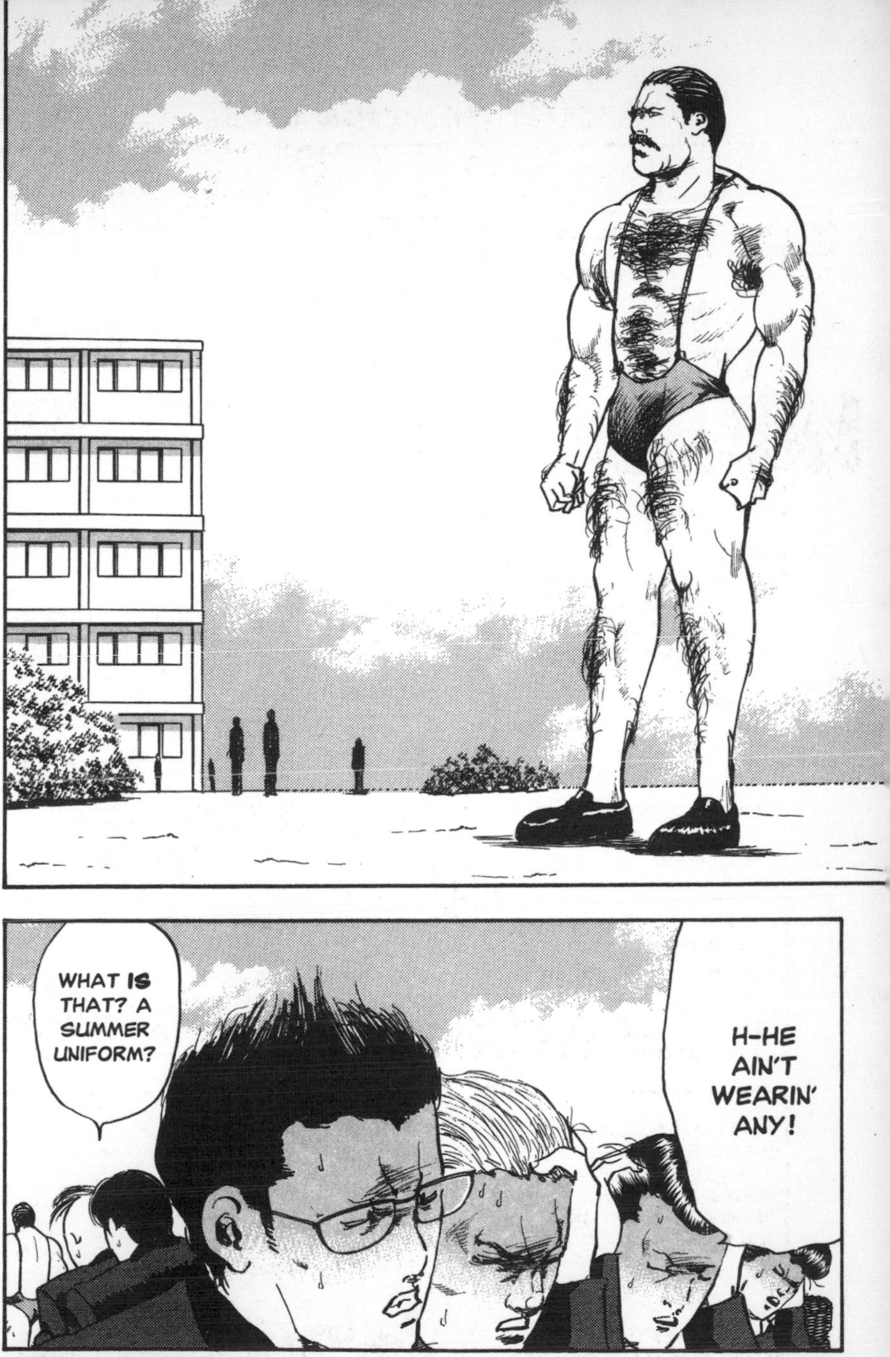
WHAT **IS** THAT? A SUMMER UNIFORM?
H-HE AIN'T WEARIN' ANY!

OF COURSE NOT.

YEAH. IT'S LIKE THERE'S SOMETHING **MISSING**. I JUST CAN'T GET PUMPED UP OVER THESE THINGS.

YOU KNOW, THESE ARE STARTING TO FEEL LESS AND LESS LIKE A SYMBOL OF STRENGTH. IT ALL SEEMS... POINTLESS SOMEHOW.

MAYBE WE SHOULD GET 'EM CLEANED FIRST.

THEN I SUGGEST WE PROCURE THE NEXT SET OF PANTS AT CROMARTIE!

IT'S 'CUZ WE STOLE ALL THESE PANTS FROM A BUNCH OF PANSY-ASSES! WE GOTTA TAKE 'EM OFF OF SOMEBODY **TOUGH**!

ME TOO! BUT WHY?!

CROMARTIE HIGH

IT'S PERFECT. C'MON, BOYS! LET'S RAISE SOME HELL!

THAT'S A PRETTY RISKY MOVE, BOSS.

YOUR PANTS ARE **OURS**!

ALRIGHT, LET'S DO IT!

DEADLY. STEALING CROMARTIE'S PANTS WILL PROVE ONCE AND FOR ALL THAT WE'RE THE STRONGEST!

YOU'RE SERIOUS ABOUT THIS, AREN'T YOU?

the stolen pants
↓

GOT A LOT OF 'EM, HUH?

BASS HIGH

HELL, YEAH! WE AIN'T SCARED OF NO ONE!

WE'RE THE STRONG-EST!

THE SHEER NUMBER OF PANTS WE'VE AMASSED IS A REFLECTION OF OUR **STRENGTH!**

BASS HIGH 1ST YEAR BOSS
JACKSON SETOUCHI

IN LAYING CLAIM TO THESE TROUSERS, WE HAVE SHOWN THE WORLD JUST HOW STRONG WE ARE.

WELL...WHAT ARE WE GONNA DO WITH ALL THESE PANTS?

ASK AWAY.

I KNOW WHERE YOU'RE COMIN' FROM, SETOUCHI... BUT THERE'S SOMETHING I GOTTA ASK.

HEY, THESE ARE STAINED!

I DON'T KNOW. DON'T THESE THINGS CARRY **DISEASES?**

YOU WANNA WEAR 'EM?

HMM.

CHAPTER FIFTY-EIGHT: **GIMME THE PRIZE**

HUH?

HEY.

fwssh

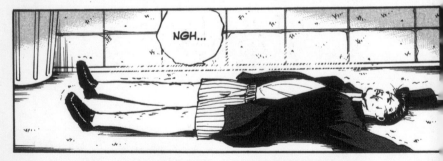

NGH...

THESE OLD-SCHOOL BADASSES WILL RENDER THEIR VICTIMS SENSELESS JUST TO STEAL THEIR TROUSERS—AN ANCIENT TACTIC, BUT ONE THAT HAS MADE A SUDDEN AND DRAMATIC COMEBACK.

PANTS POACHERS. THE WORST NIGHTMARE OF UNIFORM WEARERS EVERYWHERE.

STUDENT PROFILE   **DATE (MM/DD/YY)**

NAME	M F
Yutaka Takenouchi	

DATE OF BIRTH (MM/DD/YY)   5/5/   (AGE 16)

ADDRESS

Sipin-ku, Cromartie Street 6-4-3. Tokyo.

YEAR	MONTH	ACADEMICS/WORK EXPERIENCE
	Mar	Sipin-ku, Cromartie Elementary. Graduated.
	Mar	Sipin-ku, Cromartie Middle School. Graduated.
	Apr	Tokyo, Sipin-ku, Cromartie High School. Enrolled.

YEAR	MONTH	CERTIFICATIONS/OTHER
		Passed Level 1 of the English Proficiency Exam

ACADEMIC STRENGTHS

Everything.

PERSONAL STRENGTHS AND WEAKNESSES

Strength - Command greater respect, and fighting abilities than anyone else.

Weakness - Get carsick easily.

PEOPLE YOU ADMIRE

Bus and taxi drivers

SPECIAL SKILLS

Quantum mechanics, hitting people, English conversation

GOALS

Going by foot is always the best way to go.

INSTRUCTIONS

1. Please use blue or black ink only.   2. Please write neatly.

I wrote this (Hayashida)

STUDENT PROFILE   DATE (MM/DD/YY)

NAME		M F
Hiromi Go		

DATE OF BIRTH (MM/DD/YY)   (AGE   )

ADDRESS

YEAR	MONTH	ACADEMICS/WORK EXPERIENCE

YEAR	MONTH	CERTIFICATIONS/OTHER

ACADEMIC STRENGTHS	PERSONAL STRENGTHS AND WEAKNESSES
PEOPLE YOU ADMIRE	SPECIAL SKILLS
GOALS	

INSTRUCTIONS

1. Please use blue or black ink only.   2. Please write neatly.

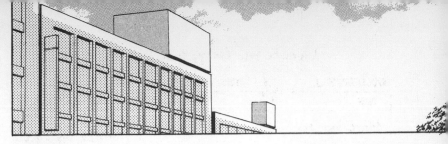

NEXT THING YOU KNOW, YOU'RE A TOTAL BADASS.

AH, THE POLICE HAVE FINALLY ARRIVED.

WOOO WOOO

THINK NOTHING OF IT! I SIMPLY DID WHAT ANYONE WOULD DO... OF COURSE, I DIDN'T REALLY **DO** MUCH OF ANYTHING.

THANKS. IS THERE SOME WAY I CAN PAY YOU BACK?

LET'S SEE. NO WEAPONS STORED IN HERE TODAY...

SAFETY COMPLIANT

LAUNCHING THAT MISSILE LAST TIME GAVE THE MISTAKEN IMPRESSION THAT I WAS A THREAT, AND SO I WAS ARRESTED. GETTING RELEASED TOOK QUITE A BIT OF WORK--I'LL HAVE TO MAKE SURE IT DOESN'T HAPPEN AGAIN.

TIRE PRESSURE IS OPTIMAL.

I MADE SURE TO WEAR MY HELMET.

HELLO, OFFICER. AS YOU CAN SEE, I HAVEN'T BROKEN A SINGLE LAW.

AND I'VE BEEN OBEYING THE SPEED LIMIT AS WELL.

VERY WELL.

I bet you got some change, too.

THAT'S IT! START JUMPIN', ASSHOLE!

YOU GOT A LOTTA NERVE...

WHAT THE HELL?!

pwshhh

WHOA!

chk

ka-chak

ka-chak

ka-thd

fwshhh

fwsssh

THERE'S SOMETHIN' SERIOUSLY WRONG WITH THIS GUY! RUN FOR IT!

stomp

stomp

H-HOLY CRAP!

PERFECT LANDING.

I KNOW YOU STILL GOT SOME CHANGE! GO ON, JUMP UP AND DOWN A BIT! I BET WE'LL HEAR SOME JINGLIN'!

HEY, YOU LISTENIN' TO ME?! I SAID GIVE ME **ALL** YER MONEY!

AIN'T NOBODY COMIN' TO HELP YOUR ASS!

grab

WHAT, YOU THINK SOMEONE'S GONNA COME RESCUE YOU? GET REAL!

glance

NOW GIVE US THE REST OF YOUR MONEY OR YOU'RE GONNA GET HURT.

THIS IS **OUR** TURF!

HUH? WHO THE HELL ARE YOU?!

vrmm

vrmm

CEASE YOUR BULLYING OF THE WEAK!

H-HE JUMPED IT!

WHAT THE HECK KIND OF MANGA IS THIS?!

OF COURSE HE WON--HE'S A FRICKIN' MOTORCYCLE! SOMEBODY DISQUALIFY THAT MORON!

HE RAN OVER TWO PEOPLE...

AND 1ST PLACE GOES TO MECHA-ZAWA-KUN!

C'MON, LIGHTEN UP. I'M SURE IT'LL ALL EVEN OUT IN THE NEXT EVENT.

OH YEAH? WELL, WHAT IF NEXT TIME HE GETS TURNED INTO A RICE COOKER OR SOMETHING? ARE YOU STILL GONNA BE ABLE TO CALL HIM YOUR FRIEND?!

YES, HE'S A BIKE...BUT UNTIL RECENTLY, HE WAS ALSO A **FRIEND**, ONE WHO WORE A UNIFORM AND CAME TO CLASS JUST LIKE THE REST OF US. I'D HAVE A REAL PROBLEM GOIN' UP TO THE GUY AND SAYING SOMETHING LIKE, "YOU'RE A MOTORCYCLE, AREN'T YOU?"

YOU SEE? HE MAY BE GOOD AT RACING EVENTS, BUT THERE'S NO WAY HE CAN BEAT US IN THE HIGH JUMP!

HE DOESN'T EVEN HAVE ANY LEGS.

HIGH JUMP, HUH?

OUR NEXT EVENT WILL BE THE HIGH JUMP.

C'MON, MECHA-ZAWA! LET'S SEE YOU TRY IT!

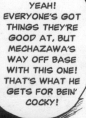

YEAH! EVERYONE'S GOT THINGS THEY'RE GOOD AT, BUT MECHAZAWA'S WAY OFF BASE WITH THIS ONE! THAT'S WHAT HE GETS FOR BEIN' COCKY!

vrm-vrm

THIS HAS GOTTA BE AGAINST THE RULES

BAM

READY!

skreee

vrrrrmmm

TRACK MEET AT CROMARTIE HIGH

MEN'S 100 METERS, 1ST HEAT

THAT'S RIGHT! THERE'S NOT A SINGLE PERSON WHO CAN OUTRUN ME!

EVER SINCE I CAME TO CROMARTIE, I HAVEN'T HAD MUCH OF A CHANCE TO STAND OUT. BUT NOW'S MY TIME TO FINALLY BE IN THE SPOTLIGHT. WHEN IT COMES TO SPRINTING, NOBODY'S FASTER THAN ME!

AKIRA MAEDA (16)

I'VE BEEN A BADASS EVER SINCE I WAS A LITTLE KID, BUT IF THERE'S ONE THING I PRIDE MYSELF ON, IT'S MY *SPEED*.

AT LEAST, THAT'S WHAT I THOUGHT...

HUH?!

vmm

rrrm

vrrrm

WHAT? BUT WHY?!

I HEARD THAT SADAHARU'S CALLIN' IT QUITS.

THE NEXT DAY

HOT-BLOODED BIKE DRAMA—THE END.

vmm

vrrrr

SO THAT WAS THE LEGENDARY SADAHARU.

HE'S GONE.

vrmmm

vrmmm

WHA...

VWOOSH

VWSHHH

IT'S **SADAHARU**! WHERE'D HE COME FROM?!

IT'S NO USE! WE'RE GIVIN' IT ALL WE GOT, AND WE STILL CAN'T KEEP UP WITH HIM!

VITTT

HE'S GOT **WAY** MORE POWER, TOO! DAMN!

I DON'T BELIEVE IT! HOW COULD HE TAKE THAT KIND OF CORNER SO FAST?! H-HE AIN'T HUMAN!

CHAPTER FIFTY-FIVE: **HIGHWAY STAR**

RIDERS COME HERE EVERY DAY IN SEARCH OF SPEED, AS WELL AS THE CHANCE TO TEST THEIR SKILLS.

KEOUGH PASS. THE SHARP CURVES OF THIS ROAD WEAVE A PATH THROUGH THE MOUNTAINS OF NORTHERN KANTO.

NOT ONLY IS HE THE FASTEST MAN KEOUGH PASS HAS EVER SEEN, BUT HIS TECHNIQUE IS NOTHING SHORT OF GENIUS. NO ONE HAS EVER OVER-TAKEN HIM—ALL WHO HAVE TRIED HAVE TASTED THE STING OF DEFEAT.

ONE OF THESE BIKERS IS A SELF-MADE LEGEND— SADAHARU!

OF COURSE HE'LL COME! HE CAN SMELL A CHALLENGE A MILE AWAY! HE'S LIKE A **WOLF!**

YOU THINK HE'LL SHOW UP TODAY?

vmmm

vmmm

NEVERTHE-LESS, THESE THREE MEN HAVE COME, HOPING TO CHALLENGE THE GREAT SADAHARU!

THAT'S RIGHT! HE ONLY GOT WHERE HE DID 'CUZ HE'S NEVER HAD A **REAL** CHALLENGE!

HEY, THERE'S NOT A MAN ALIVE WHO CAN BEAT US!

YEAH, BUT WILL WE BE GOOD ENOUGH?

*On sign: "Summer Driver's Safety Courses"

OF COURSE THEY DID.

WAUGH!

ZBWSSH

I WILL FIRE AGAIN.

AAH!

KA-BOOM

I'M NO ONE IMPORTANT. MY NAME IS NOT WORTH MENTIONING.

THANK YOU FOR ALL YOUR HELP. DO YOU MIND IF I ASK YOU YOUR NAME?

LET'S GET OUTTA HERE! WE AIN'T FORGETTIN' THIS!

THIS IS SOME UN-BELIEVABLE SHIT!

H-HE'S OUT OF HIS MIND!

BUT TOO LATE, I'M AFRAID. I HAVE ALREADY RESOLVED THE MATTER ON MY OWN.

AH, THE POLICE HAVE ARRIVED.

WOOO

WOOO

WHAT THE...

LET THE GIRL GO.

vr-vrrm

IT WOULD SEEM YOU NEED TO BE TAUGHT A LESSON.

YOU'RE GONNA PAY FOR THIS!

DON'T YOU KNOW WHO WE ARE?!

WHAT'S THE BIG IDEA, CHUMP? AND WHAT'S WITH THAT WEIRD-ASS BIKE?

pa-cht

chk

CHAPTER FIFTY-FOUR: **LETHAL WEAPON**

IF YOU DON'T STOP, I'M GOING TO SCREAM FOR HELP!

AW, WHAT'S THE BIG DEAL? HEH HEH.

PLEASE STOP!

C'MON, BABE. YOU CAN HANG OUT WITH US FOR A WHILE.

LOOK AT 'EM. THEY'RE PRETENDING NOT TO NOTICE!

GO AHEAD. SCREAM ALL YOU WANT.

YEAH, SHE'S A KEEP-ER.

HEH. THIS CHICK'S GOT SPUNK.

YOU... YOU BRUTE!

AIN'T NOBODY COMIN' TO YOUR RESCUE, SO JUST GIVE IT UP!

THIS IS **OUR** TURF! NO ONE'S GONNA TRY TO STOP US HERE!

WHO THE HECK IS THAT?!

HUH?

AUGH!

BWACK

ACTUALLY, YOU GUYS ARE KIND OF AMAZING.

OH NO!

SKRASSH!

VRRRM

DUDE, HE TOTALLY SHATTERED!

HE BROKE **AGAIN!**

WHAT DO WE DO?!

THE LAST TIME THIS HAPPENED, HE WAS REPAIRED ALMOST BEFORE WE KNEW IT. BUT THIS TIME...THE DAMAGE IS SO GREAT, I DON'T KNOW IF HE CAN BE RETURNED TO NORMAL.

UH, I DON'T THINK THAT'S THE PROBLEM HERE...

I MEANT TO SAY THIS EARLIER, BUT PEOPLE SHOULD ALWAYS WEAR THEIR HELMETS!

YEAH. NOT QUITE A FRIEND, BUT AN ACQUAINTANCE.

MECHAZAWA IS A DEAR ACQUAIN-TANCE TO BOTH OF US.

IF YOU DOUBT, THEN YOU'LL NEVER SUCCEED! YOU MUST HAVE THE WILL TO DEFY THE ODDS!

BUT... CAN WE PUT HIM BACK TO-GETHER?

WE MUST **ACT.** AND QUICKLY, BEFORE HE'S MISTAKEN FOR TRASH AND TAKEN AWAY AT THE NEXT PICKUP.

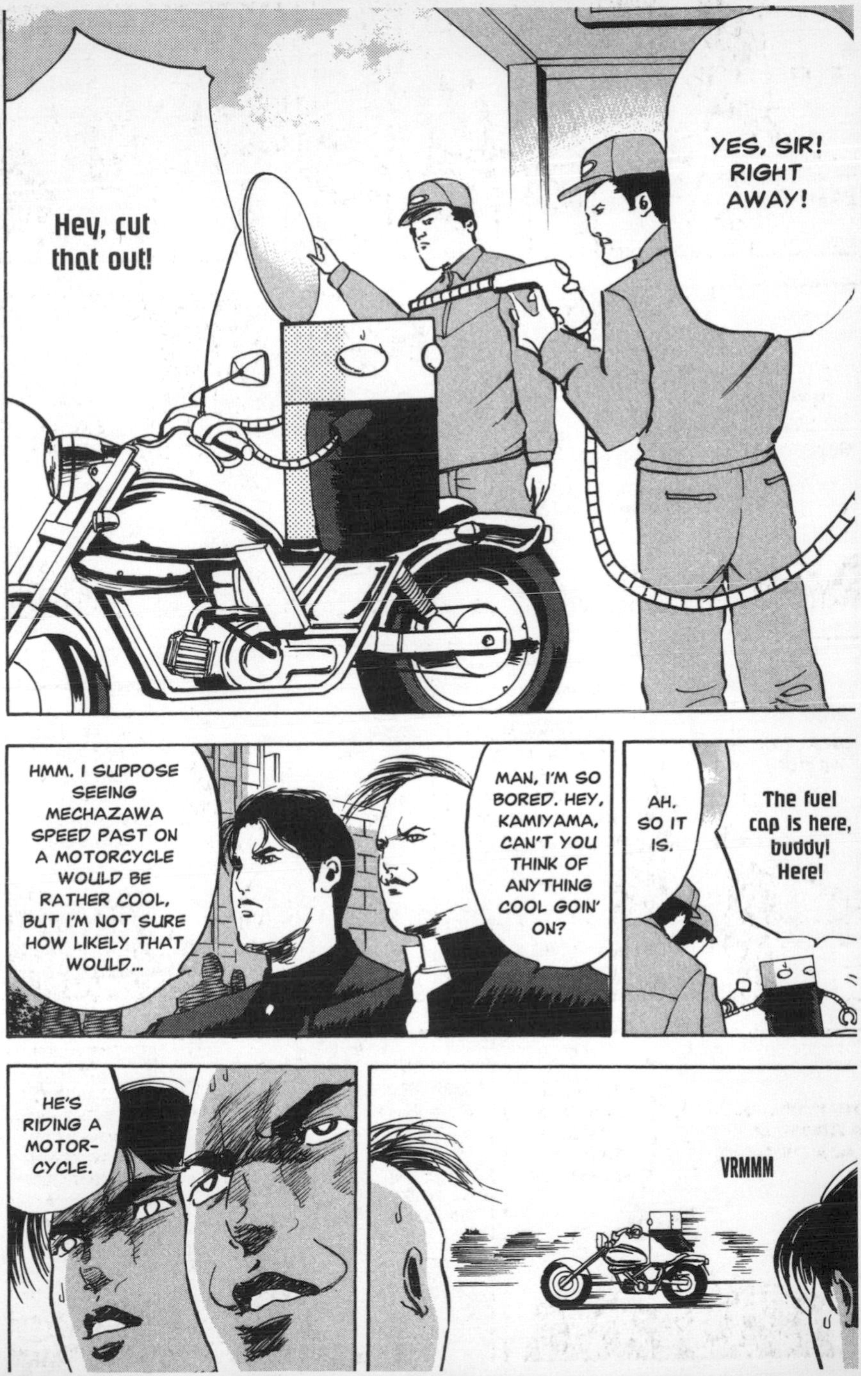

YES, SIR! RIGHT AWAY!
Hey, cut that out!
The fuel cap is here, buddy! Here!
AH. SO IT IS.
MAN, I'M SO BORED. HEY, KAMIYAMA, CAN'T YOU THINK OF ANYTHING COOL GOIN' ON?
HMM. I SUPPOSE SEEING MECHAZAWA SPEED PAST ON A MOTORCYCLE WOULD BE RATHER COOL, BUT I'M NOT SURE HOW LIKELY THAT WOULD...
VRMMM
HE'S RIDING A MOTOR-CYCLE.

CHAPTER FIFTY-THREE: **BORN TO RUN**

BRM-RM-RM-RM

I feel like I could take on the world.

But right now, it feels pretty good.

The icy breeze is piercing my skin...

vrrmmm

Goin' for a bike ride's the best way to blow off some steam.

WELCOME!

Regular

Regular Premium

Gasoline

FULL-SERVICE STATION

vrmm

Fill 'er up.

WHAT'LL IT BE, SIR?

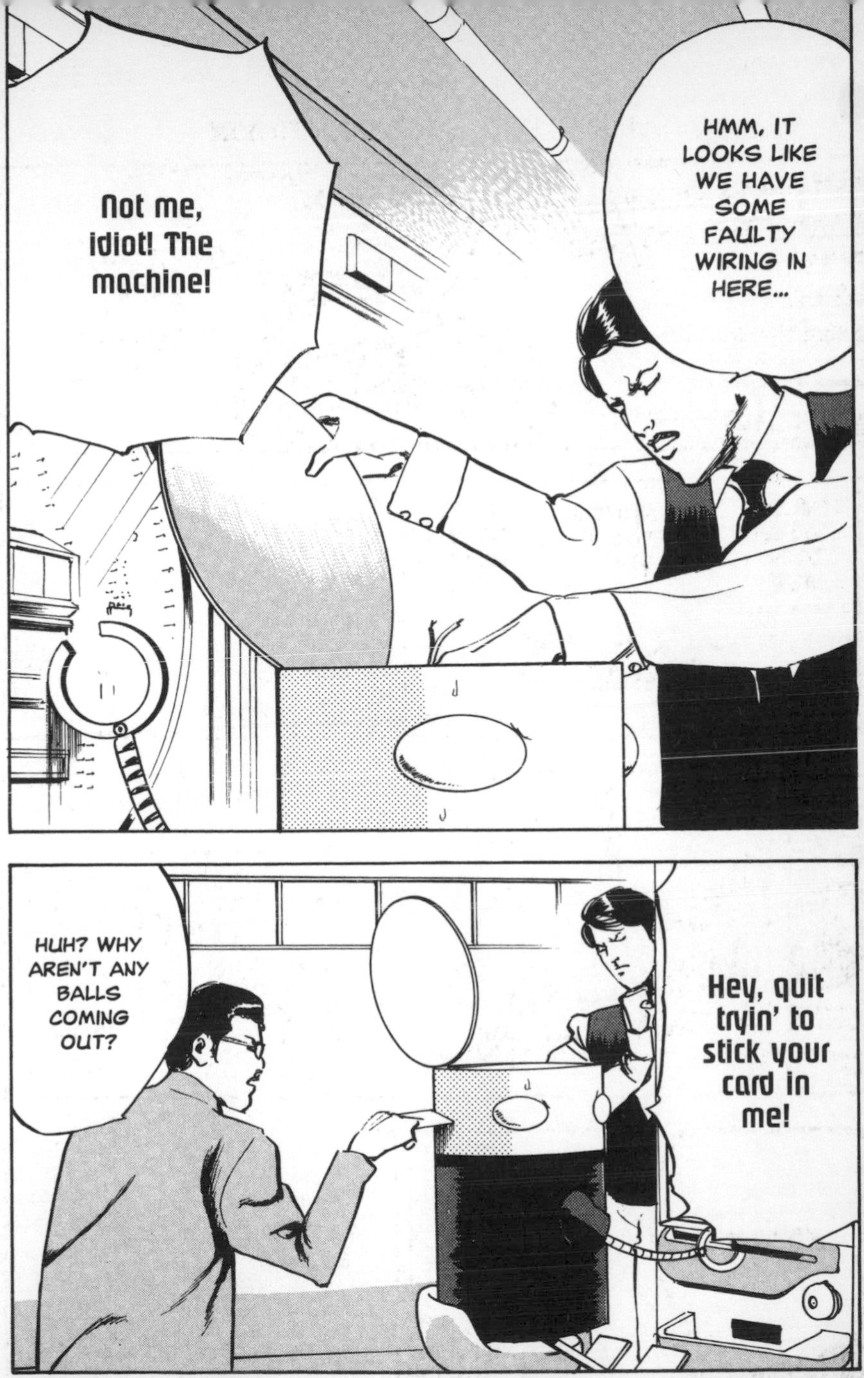
Not me, idiot! The machine!
HMM, IT LOOKS LIKE WE HAVE SOME FAULTY WIRING IN HERE...
HUH? WHY AREN'T ANY BALLS COMING OUT?
Hey, quit tryin' to stick your card in me!

NO PRIZES FOR YOU.

Man, that burns me up! I better find somethin' to take my mind off it...

Dammit, that ain't me!

YEAH, I GOT SOMETHING TO SAY! AND I'VE BEEN WANTING TO TELL YA FOR A LONG TIME!

KTNK

Hey! Where the hell're my balls?!

CHING

CHING

CL-CLNG

CL-CLNG

Ah, who cares? I've already made a mess of things today. No reason to try to fix it now.

Dammit. What am I even doing here? I was preachin' all high and mighty to those guys earlier, but now I'm starting to wonder if I even knew what I was talkin' about. Maybe I'm mad 'cuz the one who's really weak is ME.

I'M TERRIBLY SORRY, SIR. I'LL CHECK IT OUT RIGHT AWAY. WOULD YOU MIND MOVING ASIDE FOR A MOMENT?

jingle

Yeah. I got three sevens but the balls ain't coming out!

CAN I HELP YOU, SIR?

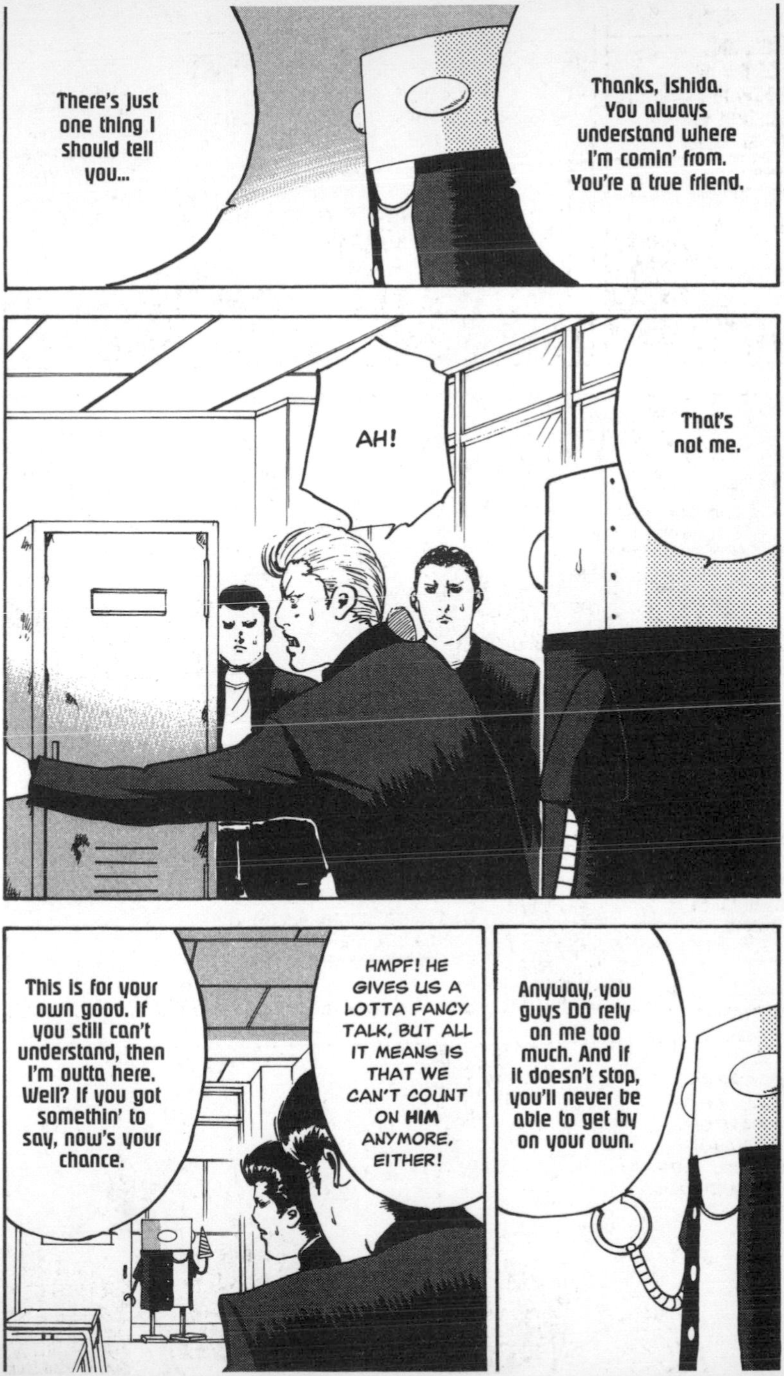

Thanks, Ishida.
You always
understand where
I'm comin' from.
You're a true friend.
There's just
one thing I
should tell
you...
That's
not me.
AH!
Anyway, you
guys DO rely
on me too
much. And if
it doesn't stop,
you'll never be
able to get by
on your own.
HMPF! HE
GIVES US A
LOTTA FANCY
TALK, BUT ALL
IT MEANS IS
THAT WE
CAN'T COUNT
ON HIM
ANYMORE,
EITHER!
This is for your
own good. If
you still can't
understand, then
I'm outta here.
Well? If you got
somethin' to
say, now's your
chance.

CHAPTER FIFTY-TWO: **BORN TO BE WILD**

WE GOT INTO IT WITH THOSE BASS GUYS THE OTHER DAY, AND NOW IT LOOKS LIKE THEY'RE PLANNING SOMETHIN' BIG. THINGS COULD START GETTIN' UGLY REAL SOON...

Yeah?

HEY, MECHA-ZAWA.

I don't know. This guy don't exactly owe me any favors. Plus, with the way things are between us and Bass right now, I don't think he'd wanna hear what I have to say.

WELL, YOU SAID YOU KNOW SOMEONE AT BASS, RIGHT? COULDN'T YOU TALK TO HIM FOR US?

And? What do you want ME to do about it?

It's like I told ya before—this is what happens when you go runnin' around trying to act all tough. You brought this on yourselves!

BUT...YOU'RE THE ONLY ONE WE CAN COUNT ON!

Sorry. I'd like to help you out, but there's only so much I can do.

MECHAZAWA'S RIGHT. WE'RE ALWAYS RUNNING TO HIM FOR HELP LIKE A BUNCH OF LITTLE KIDS! WHAT HE'S SAYIN' IS THAT WE GOTTA START TAKIN' CARE OF OUR **OWN** PROBLEMS! AIN'T THAT RIGHT, MECHAZAWA?

C'MON, YOU TWO! KNOCK IT OFF!

Oh, you want some of this?!

YOU'RE CROSSIN' THE LINE, MECHA-ZAWA!

whirrr

STUDENT PROFILE

DATE (MM/DD/YY)

NAME	(M) F
Takeshi Hokuto	

DATE OF BIRTH (MM/DD/YY) 7/7/ (AGE   )

ADDRESS

Marcano-ku, Horner Road 1-5. Tokyo.

YEAR	MONTH	ACADEMICS/WORK EXPERIENCE
	Mar	Horner City, Horner Academy Primary School. Graduated.
	Mar	Horner City, Horner Academy Middle School. Graduated.
	Apr	Horner City, Horner Academy High School. Enrolled.
		Following this, I transferred to a number of different high schools.
	Sep	Tokyo, Cromartie High School. Transferred.

YEAR	MONTH	CERTIFICATIONS/OTHER
		Have achieved 1st dan or greater in kendo, judo, traditional
		abacus, calligraphy, and so on.

ACADEMIC STRENGTHS

Sovereignty

PERSONAL STRENGTHS AND WEAKNESSES

Strength - Being the Chosen One.

Weakness - People are against me.

PEOPLE YOU ADMIRE

Napoleon, Genghis Khan, Alexander
the Great, Qin Shi Huangdi

SPECIAL SKILLS

Controlling the masses (the pigs)

Giving orders to others

GOALS

To conquer all of Japan's high schools and rule the nation.
As soon as possible.

INSTRUCTIONS

1. Please use blue or black ink only.   2. Please write neatly.

STUDENT PROFILE **DATE (MM/DD/YY)**

NAME	M / F
Akira Maeda	

DATE OF BIRTH (MM/DD/YY) 8/8/ (AGE 16)

ADDRESS

Sipin-ku, E. Wright 4-6-3. Tokyo.

YEAR	MONTH	ACADEMICS/WORK EXPERIENCE
	Mar	Sipin-ku, Krueger Elementary. Graduated.
	Mar	Sipin-ku, Racto Middle School. Graduated.
	Apr	Tokyo, Cromartie High School. Enrolled.

YEAR	MONTH	CERTIFICATIONS/OTHER
		Motorcycle license

ACADEMIC STRENGTHS

Art

PERSONAL STRENGTHS AND WEAKNESSES

Strength - Being very cool and composed.

Weakness - Having few friends and a weak presence.

PEOPLE YOU ADMIRE

My parents

SPECIAL SKILLS

Often mistaken for my mother

Often taken hostage

GOALS

Quit talking about my mother!

IT'S ALL UP TO ME NOW. I'M GONNA NEED A HILARIOUS ANSWER TO FINISH THINGS OFF WITH A BANG! I DON'T EVEN HAVE TO LISTEN TO THE QUESTION, BECAUSE IT DOESN'T MATTER **WHAT** I SAY--IT JUST HAS TO BE FUNNY!

AGAIN, THIS IS THE LAST QUESTION, SO PLEASE LISTEN CAREFULLY. HERE IN JAPAN, ABOUT 30 YEARS AGO, THERE WAS...

MY ONLY OPTION IS TO RESPOND WITH SOMETHING THAT DOESN'T NEED A COMEBACK. BUT TO GET A CHUCKLE OUT OF THESE NEANDERTHALS, I'M DEFINITELY GOING TO NEED SOMETHING LOWBROW. THAT'S IT! I'VE GOT IT!

LET'S SEE. IF IT'S AN A, B, OR C QUESTION, I COULD ANSWER "D." NAH, THAT GAG'S TOO OLD. A-HA! I COULD ANSWER **BEFORE** HE ASKS THE QUESTION! ONLY, IF HE DOESN'T HAVE A WITTY REMARK LIKE, "I HAVEN'T ASKED THE QUESTION YET," THEN THE WHOLE THING COULD FALL FLAT.

BADA-BING!

YAMA-GUCHI-SAN!

beeep

WHAT HAVE I DONE?

WHAT?! NO WAY!

CORRECT!

AND THE WINNER IS MR. YAMAGUCHI.

THE THING IS, HE MADE ME **WANT** TO DELIVER THE PUNCHLINE! THIS MOHAWK GUY IS GOOD.

WHEW, THAT WAS CLOSE! I ALMOST SHOUTED OUT, "IF YOU DON'T KNOW THE ANSWER, THEN DON'T RING THE DAMN BUZZER!" BUT I CAN'T DELIVER THE PUNCHLINE FOR HIS JOKE--THAT'D MAKE HIM LOOK GOOD AND LEAVE ME HIGH AND DRY!

HAYASHIDA-SAN!

beeep

THIRD QUESTION. WHAT IS THE TOTAL NUMBER OF MAJOR CITIES AND PREFECTURES IN JAPAN?

INCREDIBLE! HE'S PLAYING OFF HIS PREVIOUS JOKE! DOES THIS MEAN THAT HIS LAST RESPONSE WAS JUST LAYING THE GROUNDWORK FOR **THIS** ONE?! THIS GUY IS A FORCE TO BE RECKONED WITH!

NO.

YEAH, I FIGURED OUT THE ANSWER TO THAT OTHER QUESTION. CAN I TELL YOU NOW?

THIS SORT OF "TWIST" MAY BE A LITTLE CLICHED, BUT IT'S A TRIED AND TRUE ELEMENT OF THE COMEDY GAME SHOW...AND IT'S JUST WHAT'S NEEDED TO KEEP THE CONTESTANTS ON THEIR TOES! WELL DONE, HONEY BOY!

THEN WHY DID WE EVEN BOTHER WITH THEM OTHER THREE?!

HUH?!

AND NOW FOR THE FINAL QUESTION. INCIDENTALLY, THIS ONE IS WORTH THREE MILLION POINTS!

THAT IDIOT!

MAN, HE WHACKED ISHIKAWA AGAIN!

BWAP

COMEDY IS THE ANSWER! IF I EVER MAKE IT BIG, THOSE ARE THE WORDS I'LL LEAVE BEHIND FOR FUTURE GENERATIONS!

WE LIVE IN A WORLD WHERE THE "CORRECT" ANSWER DOESN'T AMOUNT TO A HILL OF BEANS! HUMOR IS WHAT'S MOST IMPORTANT! IMAGINE, SWIMSUIT MODELS TRYING TO DO COMEDY! PSH! "WONDERFUL GIRLS," INDEED!

YES, HAYASHIDA-SAN!

beeep

NEXT QUESTION. IF THE SQUARE ROOT OF 2 IS 1.4142, THEN WHAT IS 1.7320508 THE SQUARE ROOT OF?

*On hat: "Bad."

P-PERFECT! THAT'S EXACTLY THE KIND OF THING THE VIEWERS WANT TO HEAR!

COULDN'T TELL YA.

IN FACT, IT'S SO AMUSING THAT I DON'T MIND WEARING THIS SILLY TOP HAT AND PLAYING ALONG FOR A BIT!

I CAME HERE TO BEAT THE CRAP OUT OF HIM, BUT SOMEHOW I'VE ENDED UP ON A GAME SHOW INSTEAD. WELL DONE, HONEY BOY! THIS IS A MOST AMUSING TURN OF EVENTS.

OK, FIRST QUESTION!

WE CAME HERE TO KICK **YOUR** ASS! HOW CAN YOU BE THE FRICKIN' HOST?!

FINE. I GUESS WE GOTTA, LIKE, RELENT AND DO THIS QUIZ THING. BUT STILL...

THE SO-CALLED "WONDERFUL GIRLS" OF THE HIT TV SHOW *WONDERFUL* ARE NOT THE ORIGINAL MEMBERS. HOW MANY CAST ROTATIONS HAVE THESE GIRLS BEEN THROUGH?

AH, DODGING POINTLESS QUESTIONS THAT DON'T FURTHER THE STORY. YOU REALLY ARE SOMETHING, HONEY BOY! YOU HAVE AN EXCELLENT FEEL FOR CONTINUITY AS WELL AS HUMOR.

YES!

CORRECT.

F-FOUR!

beeep

LET US BEGIN!

NOW THEN.

WHAT? A QUIZ?!

WHEN YOU KNOW THE ANSWER, PLEASE PRESS THE BUZZER AS QUICKLY AS YOU CAN.

KINGPIN QUIZ SERIES "All Across America"

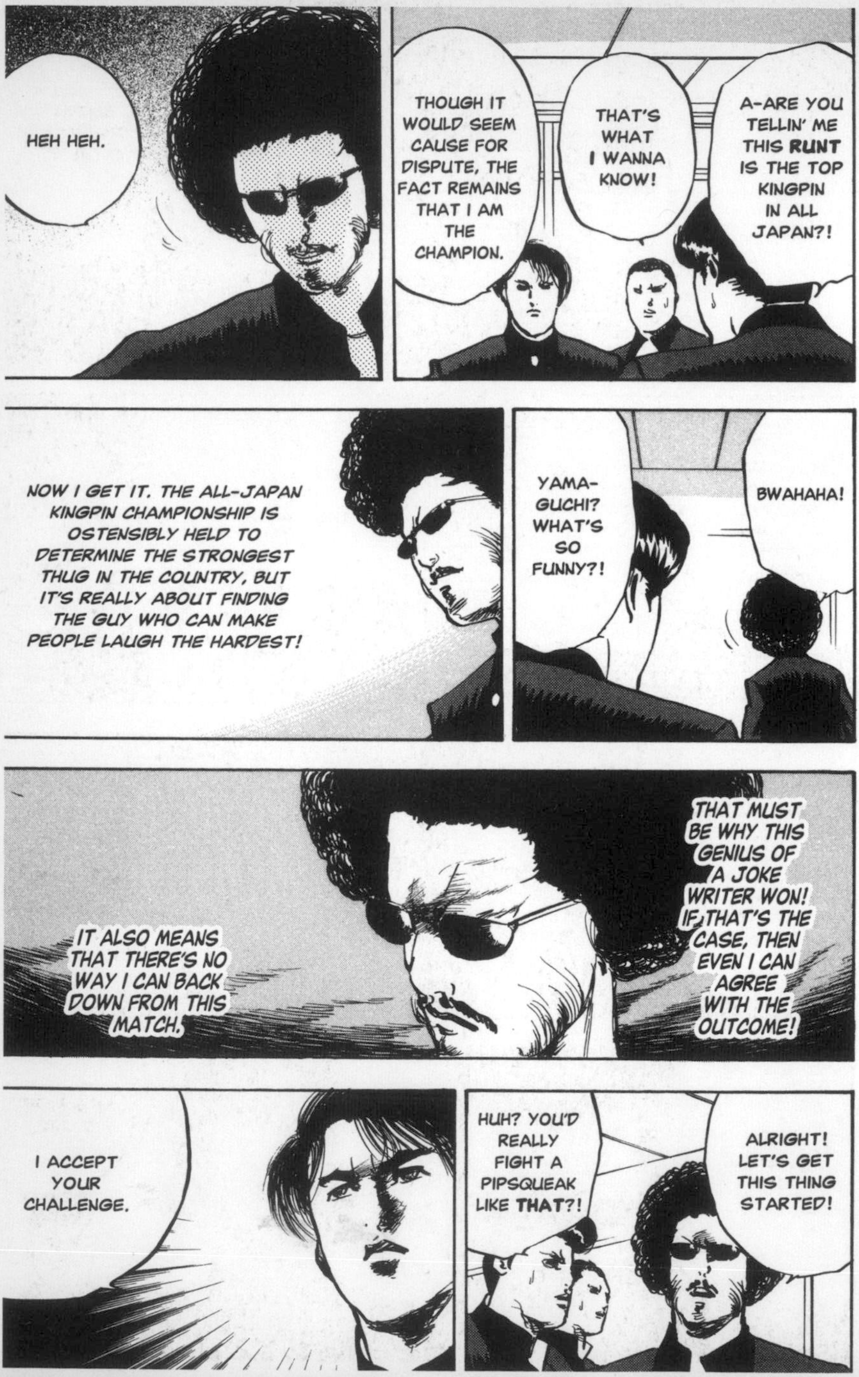
A-ARE YOU TELLIN' ME THIS **RUNT** IS THE TOP KINGPIN IN ALL JAPAN?!
THAT'S WHAT I WANNA KNOW!
THOUGH IT WOULD SEEM CAUSE FOR DISPUTE, THE FACT REMAINS THAT I AM THE CHAMPION.
HEH HEH.
BWAHAHA!
YAMA-GUCHI? WHAT'S SO FUNNY?!
NOW I GET IT. THE ALL-JAPAN KINGPIN CHAMPIONSHIP IS OSTENSIBLY HELD TO DETERMINE THE STRONGEST THUG IN THE COUNTRY, BUT IT'S REALLY ABOUT FINDING THE GUY WHO CAN MAKE PEOPLE LAUGH THE HARDEST!
THAT MUST BE WHY THIS GENIUS OF A JOKE WRITER WON! IF THAT'S THE CASE, THEN EVEN I CAN AGREE WITH THE OUTCOME!
IT ALSO MEANS THAT THERE'S NO WAY I CAN BACK DOWN FROM THIS MATCH.
ALRIGHT! LET'S GET THIS THING STARTED!
HUH? YOU'D REALLY FIGHT A PIPSQUEAK LIKE **THAT**?!
I ACCEPT YOUR CHALLENGE.

RATTLE

OUTTA THE WAY, CHUMPS!

WE HEARD YOU PUNKS GOT THE #1 KINGPIN IN JAPAN HERE.

WHAT THE HELL DO YOU THINK YOU'RE DOIN' HERE?!

HEY, THOSE GUYS ARE FROM DESTRADE!

HUH?!

I AM YAMAGUCHI! BRING OUT THIS "STRONGEST KINGPIN" OF YOURS! AFTER I KICK HIS ASS, THAT TITLE WILL BE MINE!

OUR BOSS, YAMAGUCHI, WANTS TO GO ONE-ON-ONE WITH HIM!

IT'S HONEY BOY!

I'M YOUR MAN.

HE'S RIGHT THERE.

TAKASHI KAMIYAMA
(AKA "HONEY BOY")

CHAPTER FIFTY-ONE: **THE SHOW MUST GO ON**

HEY, DID YOU GUYS HEAR ABOUT THE KINGPIN CHAMPIONSHIP? THEY'RE SAYIN' SOME GUY FROM CROMARTIE WON!

DESTRADE HIGH

A COUPLE OF LOSERS GET TOGETHER AND THINK THEY CAN DECIDE THE TOP KINGPIN IN JAPAN? AND THEY DON'T TELL US ABOUT IT?! WHAT A BUNCH OF CRAP!

WAIT A DAMN MINUTE! I AIN'T NEVER HEARD OF NO KINGPIN CONTEST!

I HEARD IT WAS OVER IN LESS THAN AN HOUR!

IT WAS A CROMARTIE GUY WHO WON, RIGHT? SO ALL I HAFTA DO IS GO OVER THERE AND KICK HIS ASS.

YAMA-GUCHI...

EASY THERE.

NOBORU YAMAGUCHI

YAMAGUCHI: REGULAR CONTRIBUTOR TO VARIOUS LATE-NIGHT COMEDY RADIO PROGRAMS. HAS NAMED KAMIYAMA AS HIS RIVAL.

1 - 2

CROMARTIE

CROMARTIE HIGH

I'M OUTTA HERE.

ALRIGHT! YAMAGU-CHI'S MAKIN' HIS MOVE!

THE ANSWER IS "TRUE."

Kamiyama →

I-IT CAN'T BE OVER! NOT AFTER ONE FRICKIN' ROUND!

OUR WINNER IS MR. KAMIYAMA FROM CROMARTIE HIGH SCHOOL!

OF COURSE IT'S A DAIRY PRODUCT.

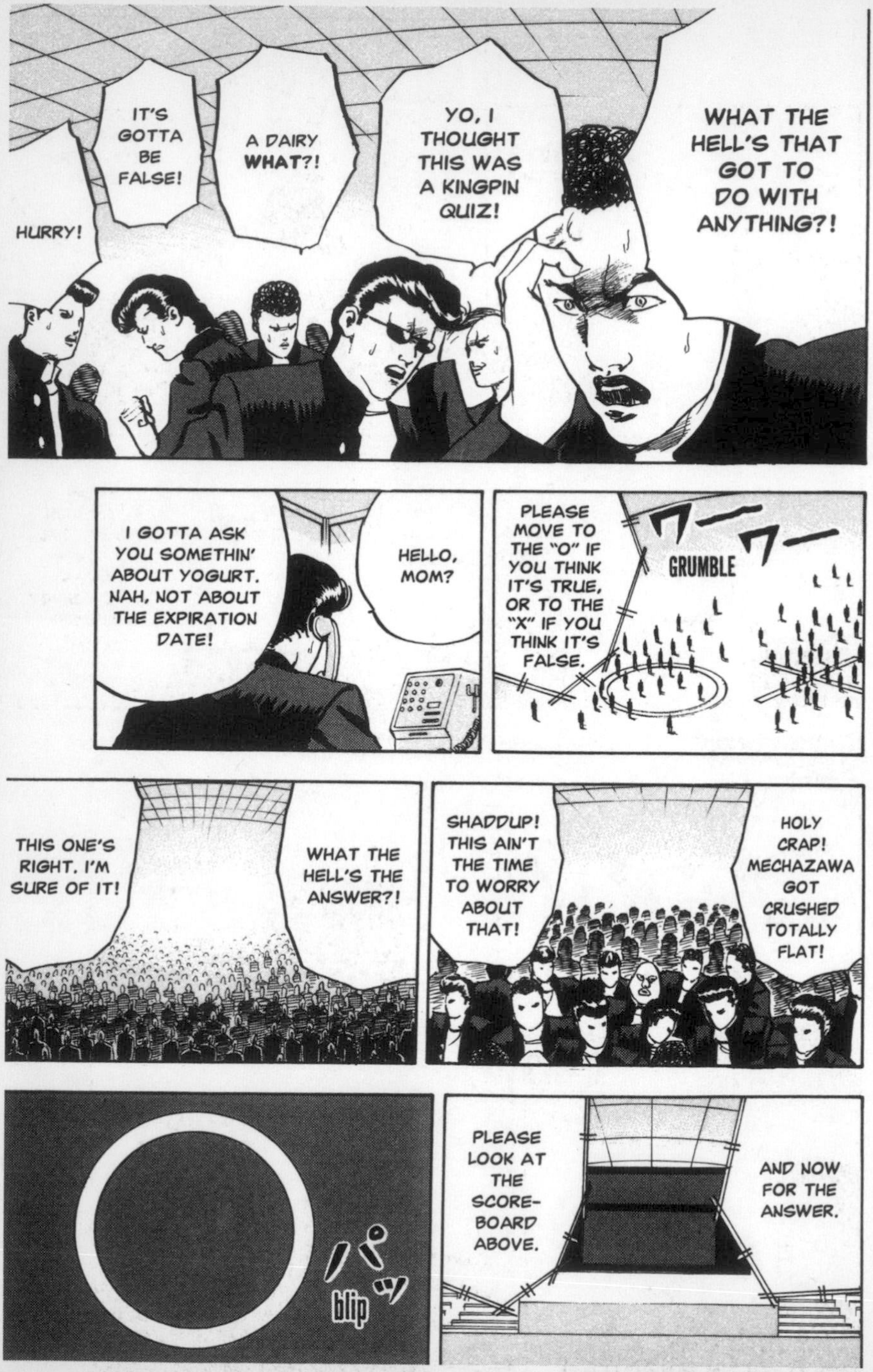
WHAT THE HELL'S THAT GOT TO DO WITH ANYTHING?!
YO, I THOUGHT THIS WAS A KINGPIN QUIZ!
A DAIRY WHAT?!
IT'S GOTTA BE FALSE!
HURRY!
ワー ワー
GRUMBLE
PLEASE MOVE TO THE "O" IF YOU THINK IT'S TRUE, OR TO THE "X" IF YOU THINK IT'S FALSE.
HELLO, MOM?
I GOTTA ASK YOU SOMETHIN' ABOUT YOGURT. NAH, NOT ABOUT THE EXPIRATION DATE!
HOLY CRAP! MECHAZAWA GOT CRUSHED TOTALLY FLAT!
SHADDUP! THIS AIN'T THE TIME TO WORRY ABOUT THAT!
WHAT THE HELL'S THE ANSWER?!
THIS ONE'S RIGHT. I'M SURE OF IT!
AND NOW FOR THE ANSWER.
PLEASE LOOK AT THE SCORE-BOARD ABOVE.
パッ
blip

I'M LOOKIN' FORWARD TO IT!

SEE YA AT THE FINALS!

LOOK, ALL I'M SAYIN' IS THAT THERE'S ALL KINDS OF WILD GUYS HERE!

BUT...DOESN'T THAT MEAN HE JUST LIKES ANIMALS?

IT'S FINALLY STARTIN'!

WHOOOAA

YOUR ATTENTION PLEASE! THE ALL-JAPAN KINGPIN CHAMPIONSHIP WILL NOW BEGIN!

QUESTION NUMBER ONE!

TRUE OR FALSE: YOGURT IS A "DAIRY PRODUCT."

HEY, LOOK!

WHOA, CHECK IT OUT!

THEY SAY HE CHALLENGED A BEAR TO A FIGHT AND WON!

THAT'S KASHIWA-BARA THE BEAR KILLER FROM HOKKAIDO!

I DON'T KNOW HOW STRONG HE IS, BUT HE'S GOTTA BE ONE BAD DUDE!

SO... DOES THAT MEAN HE'S STRONG?

I HEARD HE CAN **TALK** TO BEARS!

IT'S "HE KILLS EVERYONE" TAKASHIRO FROM NIIGATA!

THEY SAY HE **RAISES** BEARS AT HOME!

IT'S OKAJI THE OVERLY FLATTERING!

GOOD GOD, LOOK OVER THERE!

WHAT THE HELL BOOK IS THAT?!

TRYIN' TO GET A LEG UP, HUH? OK, LET'S SEE...

WHAT KINDA STUFF DID THEY ASK IN THE QUIZ LAST YEAR?

• • • • • •

TRUE OR FALSE: A KINGPIN IS **NOT** THE SAME AS A LYNCHPIN.

COUNT ME IN, TOO!

THAT STUFF'S EASY! BRING IT ON!

YEAH. I DON'T KNOW THE ANSWER, BUT IT'S ALL ABOUT KINGPINS ALRIGHT.

THAT'S FRIGGIN' INCREDIBLE! IT REALLY **IS** A TEST FOR KINGPINS!

AND, THIS IS WHERE IT WAS HELD.

THE DAY OF THE COMPETITION CAME AT LAST...

A TRUE KINGPIN NEEDS BRAINS, BRAWN, AND A LITTLE LUCK! IDIOTS, UNLUCKY SONS OF BITCHES, AND OTHER LOSERS JUST WON'T CUT IT!

SURE A GUY CAN BE TOUGH, BUT IT TAKES MORE THAN THAT TO BE A KINGPIN!

I COULDN'T TELL YA.

BY THE WAY, WHO SPONSORS THIS THING?

DAMN, THEY REALLY THOUGHT THIS THING OUT! THIS CONTEST IS **DEEP**!

I GET IT. SO THE QUIZ IS TO WEED OUT ALL THE WANNABES.

WHAT?! BUT IT'S BEEN OVER 50 YEARS!

THEY'VE BEEN DOIN' IT EVER SINCE THE END OF THE WAR... AND THEY HAVEN'T FOUND ANYONE WORTHY OF THE TITLE YET.

BUT WHOEVER THEY ARE, THEY'RE OUT TO FIND THE BIGGEST KINGPIN IN ALL JAPAN.

YEAH, WHAT?

UH, CAN I ASK YOU A QUESTION?

ANYWAY! THE QUIZ IS ONLY THE FIRST PART OF THE COMPETITION. AFTER THAT, EVERYONE WHO'S LEFT HAS GOTTA DIG IN AND **FIGHT**!

FIRST, THEY START THINGS OFF WITH A TRUE OR FALSE QUIZ.

ABOUT **HALF** THE COMPETITION GETS ELIMINATED IN THIS ROUND.

YOU GUYS DON'T HAVE A CLUE, DO YA?

IN A FIGHT, IT'S ALL ABOUT HOW TOUGH YOU ARE! WHAT THE HELL USE IS A QUIZ?!

YEAH! THIS IS SUPPOSED TO BE ABOUT WHO'S THE STRONGEST **KINGPIN**, NOT THE FRICKIN' QUIZ KING!

HEY, WHAT DOES THAT GOTTA DO WITH BEIN' TOUGH?!

Y-YEAH, I GET IT NOW.

YOU SEE? HOW **STRONG** YOU ARE HAS GOT NOTHIN' TO DO WITH IT!

OBVIOUSLY, HE GOES TO THE HOSPITAL FOR SURGERY. AND HE'S NOT GONNA BE DOIN' ANY FIGHTING FOR A WHILE!

IMAGINE THERE'S THIS INSANELY STRONG DUDE, BUT RIGHT BEFORE AN IMPORTANT FIGHT HE GOES AND GETS APPENDICITIS! WHAT THEN?!

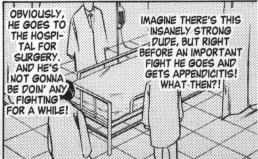

I HEARD THAT NO ONE WHO'S ENTERED THAT COMPETITION HAS MADE IT BACK ALIVE.

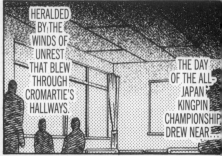

HERALDED BY THE WINDS OF UNREST THAT BLEW THROUGH CROMARTIE'S HALLWAYS.

THE DAY OF THE ALL-JAPAN KINGPIN CHAMPIONSHIP DREW NEAR...

L-LIKE WHAT?

NAH, THERE ARE **SOME** RULES.

YOU MEAN THERE AIN'T ANY RULES?!

THEY SAY IT'S TOTALLY NO HOLDS BARRED.

NO WAY! IT'S THAT TOUGH?

THE THING IS, THERE'S NO LIMIT TO THE NUMBER OF PEOPLE WHO CAN COMPETE. CROMARTIE GOT INVITED, SO THEORETICALLY **ALL OF US** COULD ENTER.

HUH? YOUR **CARD**?

What the heck?

FOR STARTERS, EVERYONE'S GOTTA BE THERE BY 8:00 AM. AND IF YOU DIDN'T MAIL YOUR REGISTRATION CARD IN TIME, YOU'RE OUT!

LISTEN UP. YOU MIGHT LEARN SOMETHING.

YEAH, RIGHT! THERE'S NO WAY THEY'D FIND A WINNER WITH SO MANY PEOPLE COMPETIN'!

SNUBBED EVEN BY HIS LACKEY...

THAT'S RIGHT! THE MAN IS **WORLD-CLASS**!

NOT IN HIS LEAGUE?! WAIT A MINUTE. ARE YOU SAYING...

YOU GUYS WERE JUST TALKING ABOUT THAT ALL-JAPAN KINGPIN THING, RIGHT? AS FAR AS HOKUTO-SAN IS CONCERNED, THAT THING'S NOT EVEN IN HIS LEAGUE!

I HAD NO IDEA. DAMN, HOKUTO, YOU ROCK!

I don't really get it.

YOU MEAN, HE WANTS TO BE THE #1 KINGPIN IN THE WORLD?!

UNLIKE YOU ALL, HE IS NOT CONTENT TO SETTLE FOR BEING THE KINGPIN OF JAPAN!

WHAT?

LET ME ASK YOU SOMETHING.

WE'RE GETTING OFF TRACK AGAIN.

IT SEEMS...

HMM. THIS IS HARDLY MY AREA OF EXPERTISE, BUT THERE IS ONE THING I CAN SAY FOR CERTAIN...

MY GOAL IS TO BE KINGPIN OF THE WORLD, BUT WHERE DO YOU THINK WOULD BE A GOOD PLACE TO START?

YOU'RE NOT GONNA ENTER, ARE YA?

BUT JUST SO I KNOW, WHAT'S THE PRIZE?

I FOR ONE AM AGAINST SUCH AN INHERENTLY VIOLENT COMPETITION!

I-IT'S HOKUTO!

HMPH! CRETINS.

THIS TOURNAMENT'S A BIG DEAL, CHUMP. WE NEED SOMEONE WHO'S BAD ENOUGH TO REPRESENT ALL OF TOKYO.

HOLD IT A SECOND! IT SEEMS TO ME YOU DON'T UNDERSTAND JUST HOW **AWESOME** HOKUTO-SAN REALLY IS! IF YOU'D LET ME EXPLAIN...

WHAT?

WE'RE KINDA BUSY RIGHT NOW. DO US A FAVOR AND SCRAM, WILL YA?

UH...

OH YEAH? **HOW** HUGE?

WELL, FOR STARTERS... HIS SHEER MAGNITUDE! I MEAN, YOU GUYS ARE NOTHING COMPARED TO HIM! THE MAN'S HUGE!

ALRIGHT, THEN. WHAT MAKES HIM SO "AWE-SOME"?

ON THE OTHER HAND, GOING TO THOSE CRETINS AND ASKING THEIR **PERMISSION** TO COMPETE IS OUT OF THE QUESTION. MY PRIDE WOULD NEVER ALLOW IT.

YOU KNOW, THE FACT THAT NEITHER OF US WERE INVITED IS A FAILING THAT CANNOT BE IGNORED!

WE CAN TRY ONE MORE TIME TO CONVINCE THEM OF YOUR AWESOMENESS. WHEN THOSE IDIOTS FINALLY REALIZE HOW IMPORTANT YOU ARE, THEY'LL BEG YOU TO BE IN THE COMPETITION!

WELL, HOW ABOUT THIS?

IS THERE ANYTHING YOU CAN THINK OF?

1 - 2

YOU JUST LEAVE THAT TO ME.

YES, BUT THE HARD PART WILL BE EXPLAINING THE SHEER **MAGNITUDE** OF MY CHARACTER IN A WAY THAT EVEN THOSE MORONS CAN UNDERSTAND.

AN OMINOUS AND BROODING ATMOSPHERE PERMEATED THE CLASSROOMS.

BY THIS TIME, ALL DISCUSSION CENTERED ON THE CHAMPIONSHIP.

YOU DON'T SAY.

STILL, EVEN IF I **HAD** GONE, I'M NOT ESPECIALLY FOND OF SINGING.

YOU KNOW, I REALLY SHOULD HAVE GONE WITH THEM TO KARAOKE. MY REFUSAL WILL ONLY MAKE IT HARDER FOR THEM TO INVITE ME NEXT TIME.

BUT WHENEVER PEOPLE DO KARAOKE IN A GROUP, THERE'S ALWAYS SOME HALF-WIT WHO PUSHES THE MIC IN EVERYONE'S FACE, DEMANDING THAT THEY SING. AND IF YOU REFUSE, IT WILL ONLY MAKE THINGS AWKWARD.

OF COURSE, I DON'T HAVE A PROBLEM LISTENING TO **OTHER** PEOPLE SING. I ENJOY A GOOD SONG AS MUCH AS THE NEXT GUY.

THE THING IS, I'M NOT A BAD SINGER. SURE, THERE ARE PEOPLE WHO'D JUMP TO THAT CONCLUSION, BUT THE FACT OF THE MATTER IS I **DO** HAVE A GOOD VOICE. I'M JUST NOT ALTOGETHER FOND OF SINGING.

UH... RIGHT.

I WOULD NEVER DO THAT, THOUGH. I'M SENSITIVE TO OTHER PEOPLE'S FEELINGS.

YES, I KNOW. I APOLOGIZE FOR GETTING US OFF THE SUBJECT.

THE **KINGPIN** CHAMPIONSHIP. NOT A KARAOKE COMPETITION...

OF COURSE.

SO...YOU'LL BE GOING TO THE CHAMPIONSHIP THEN?

INSOLENT WORM!

SEE, NOW THAT'S WHY YOU HAVE TROUBLE MAKING FRIENDS.

I MEAN, SILENCE! DON'T PRESUME TO INCLUDE ME AMONG THE RANKS OF YOU **COMMONERS**!

I, ON THE OTHER HAND, WILL ONE DAY BE **RULER** OF THIS LAND! I HAVE NO NEED FOR SUCH TAWDRY ACQUAINTANCES!

THE YEARNING FOR FRIEND-SHIP IS AN EMOTION FELT BY THE MOST PITIABLE OF FOOLS!

OF COURSE.

SO...WILL YOU BE ENTERING THE COMPETI-TION?

GOOD.

I SEE.

ME? NO, I'VE JUST HEARD OTHER PEOPLE TALKING ABOUT IT.

WELL, WEREN'T **YOU** INVITED?

BUT YOU WEREN'T INVITED, WERE YOU? I DON'T KNOW IF YOU CAN JUST WALTZ UP THERE AND SAY, "I WANNA COMPETE."

WELL... MAYBE IT'S BECAUSE YOU DON'T HANG OUT WITH YOUR FRIENDS VERY MUCH.

WHY WAS I NOT INFORMED OF THIS SOONER?

HOW CARELESS OF ME NOT TO HAVE KNOWN OF SUCH AN EVENT!

NONSENSE! I HAVE LOTS OF FRIENDS!

I'LL BE HONEST WITH YOU-- YOU'RE LOSING YOUR FRIENDS.

LIKE LAST TIME, WHEN EVERYONE WENT TO KARAOKE AFTER SCHOOL. YOU SAID YOU FELT LIKE WATCHING TV, SO YOU JUST WENT HOME.

UM...

LIKE WHO?

HMM. I SUPPOSE I DON'T HAVE ANY "FRIENDS" PER SE. PERHAPS I SHOULD START GOING TO KARAO...

I MEAN, I'M MORE OF AN ASSOCIATE THAN A FRIEND.

YOU'RE COUNTING ME AS A FRIEND?!

WELL, THERE'S YOU.

CHAPTER FORTY-NINE: **ENTER THE HOKUTO**

MONEY, POLITICAL STRENGTH, PHYSICAL PROWESS--I POSSESS ALL OF THESE. INDEED, ONE COULD SAY I WAS BORN TO BE A RULER OF MEN! BY THE WAY, I MISTAKENLY TRANSFERRED TO CROMARTIE HIGH SCHOOL.

MY NAME IS TAKESHI HOKUTO. MY FAMILY OWNS JAPAN'S FOREMOST ZAIBATSU CONGLOMERATE, THE HOKUTO FOUNDATION. WHAT'S MORE, MY SKILLS IN THE MARTIAL ARTS ARE BEYOND COMPARE.

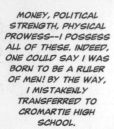

HAVE YOU EVER HEARD OF THE KINGPIN CHAMPION- SHIP?

WELL, WHAT IS IT?

HOKUTO- SAN! I'VE GOT SOME BIG NEWS!

YOU MEAN...IT WILL DETERMINE THE MOST POWERFUL MASTERMIND IN THE ENTIRE COUNTRY?!

IT'S A CONTEST TO DECIDE THE **KING** OF ALL KINGPINS!

PSHHH

WHAT ARE YOU TALKING ABOUT?

REPRESENTATIVES FROM EACH OF JAPAN'S DELINQUENT SCHOOLS GATHER TO COMPETE IN THIS EVENT, WHICH IS HELD ONCE A YEAR (SAVE FOR A BRIEF HIATUS DURING THE OIL CRISIS OF THE 1970s). AS THE DAY OF THE COMPETITION DRAWS NEAR, IT INVARIABLY BECOMES THE HOT TOPIC IN THE HALLS OF CROMARTIE.

THE ALL-JAPAN KINGPIN CHAMPIONSHIP IS INDEED A COMPETITION TO DECIDE THE MIGHTIEST OF KINGPINS!

STUDENT PROFILE   DATE (MM/DD/YY)

NAME   (M) F

Shinjiro Hayashida

DATE OF BIRTH (MM/DD/YY)   12/25   (AGE)

ADDRESS

Sipin-ku, S. Kruger 102, 5-24-17. Tokyo.

YEAR	MONTH	ACADEMICS/WORK EXPERIENCE
	Apr	Osaka, Bucky Academy Primary School. Enrolled.
		Fukuoka, Mitchell-shi, Hakutenjin Elementary. Transferred.
		Tokyo, Sipin-ku, Cromartie Elementary. Transferred.
	Mar	Tokyo, Sipin-ku, Cromartie Elementary. Graduated.
	Mar	Tokyo, Sipin-ku, Cromartie Middle School. Graduated.
	Apr	Tokyo, Cromartie High School. Enrolled.

YEAR	MONTH	CERTIFICATIONS/OTHER
		Driver's license (for my moped).

ACADEMIC STRENGTHS

None

PERSONAL STRENGTHS AND WEAKNESSES

Strength - Cheerful personality.

Totally
Weakness - Not focused.

PEOPLE YOU ADMIRE

Antonio Inoki

SPECIAL SKILLS

Boxing, golf, jazz

GOALS

I want to go to the Koshien baseball championship!

INSTRUCTIONS

1. Please use blue or black ink only.   2. Please write neatly.

STUDENT PROFILE DATE (MM/DD/YY)

NAME	Ⓜ F
Takashi Kamiyama	

DATE OF BIRTH (MM/DD/YY) 6/27/ (AGE 16)

ADDRESS

Ponce-ku, West Sheets 4-16-3. Tokyo.

YEAR	MONTH	ACADEMICS/WORK EXPERIENCE
	Mar	Ponce-ku, Paciorek Elementary School (East). Graduated.
	Mar	Ponce-ku, Paciorek Middle School. Graduated.
	Apr	Tokyo, Cromartie High School. Enrolled.

YEAR	MONTH	CERTIFICATIONS/OTHER

ACADEMIC STRENGTHS

All areas of study.
Only weakness is P.E.

PERSONAL STRENGTHS AND WEAKNESSES

Strength - Helping others to walk the high road.

Weakness - Sometimes make substantial errors in judgment.

PEOPLE YOU ADMIRE

"Beat" Takeshi
"Beat" Kiyoshi

SPECIAL SKILLS

-Help resolve disputes between others.
-Regularly contribute to late-night radio programs.

GOALS

Actually, my biggest goal is to transfer out of here as soon as possible.

*On shirt: "Birthday."

AND WHY DID HE HAVE A DRILL ON HIS HAND?

I'LL GO GET A BANANA TO LURE HIM AWAY. TRY TO HOLD YOUR OWN FOR A LITTLE WHILE, ALRIGHT?

SHOOT! HE SPOTTED ME!

WHAT?! I NEVER IMAGINED THAT **THIS** IS HOW YOU'D BE SEEING THE LIGHT!

HE'S GOING THROUGH IT PRETTY QUICK, TOO. I CAN ALREADY LOOK OUT THROUGH THE HOLE HE'S MADE.

Yeah, thanks.

BE GRATEFUL, PEON.

HEY, HOKUTO GOT YOU A WHITE UNIFORM JUST LIKE HIS!

OK, IT'S TIME FOR THE PRESENTS!

NO, WAIT! THERE'S STILL ONE INCREDIBLY SURPRISING...UH, I MEAN, AREN'T YOU ALL FORGETTING SOMETHING?

THAT JUST ABOUT WRAPS IT UP, HUH?

Thanks.

HAPPY BIRTHDAY.

AND TAKENOUCHI GOT YOU A MASK!

THAT'S RIGHT! MECHAZAWA-KUN, IF YOU WOULD DO THE HONORS!

HEY, YEAH! THE CAKE'S, LIKE, THE MOST IMPORTANT PART!

YOU MEAN THE CAKE?

THEY'RE CALLING FOR AN ENCORE.

DON'T LOSE HEART! JUST HANG IN THERE A LITTLE LONGER AND YOU **WILL** SEE THE LIGHT!

MAYBE WE SHOULD JUST GIVE UP ON THE CAKE IDEA.

HE'S ACTUALLY QUITE GOOD.

LOOK BEHIND YOU.

WHAT DO YOU MEAN?

UH, KAMIYAMA? I THINK WE HAVE A PROBLEM.

WHAT?! THIS IS MOST UNEXPECTED!

THE GORILLA'S EATING THE CAKE.

IT SEEMS I'VE RUN INTO SOME UNEXPECTED COMPETITION--AND NOT JUST FROM FREDDIE, EITHER. THERE'S A WHOLE BUNCH OF REALLY INTERESTING PEOPLE HERE TODAY...

GOOD. WE'LL TALK LATER.

I GUESS I'LL JUST WAIT UNTIL HE'S DONE SINGING, THEN.

IT'S KAMIYAMA. THERE'S SOMETHING I THOUGHT I SHOULD TELL YOU.

HELLO?

rrring

Hey, thanks guys.

HAPPY BIRTH-DAY!

COME TO THINK OF IT, WHAT COULD BE MORE INTERESTING THAN MECHA-ZAWA'S *BIRTHDAY*?!

UH, WHY NOT START WITH THE GOOD NEWS?

WHICH WOULD YOU LIKE TO HEAR FIRST?

WHAT? GOOD NEWS **AND** BAD NEWS?

ACTUALLY, I'VE GOT GOOD NEWS AND BAD NEWS.

THE BAD NEWS IS...

THAT **IS** GOOD NEWS. SO, WHAT'S THE BAD NEWS?

fwee!

clap

clap

woo-hoo!

clap

VERY WELL. THE GOOD NEWS IS THAT FREDDIE'S DONE SINGING.

ABOUT THIS PLAN...I WAS SUPPOSED TO JUMP OUTTA THE CAKE AFTER MECHAZAWA BLOWS OUT THE CANDLES, BUT I'VE BEEN THINKING. MAYBE THERE'S NO NEED TO BE SO PARTICULAR ABOUT **WHEN** I DO IT.

IT'S ME. I'M CALLING FROM INSIDE THE CAKE.

HELLO?

WHAT? WHY NOT?

NOW'S NOT A GOOD TIME, THOUGH.

I SEE. SO YOU'RE SAYING THE CAKE LEAPING, IF YOU WILL, SHOULD BE PERFORMED AT THE BEST POSSIBLE MOMENT INSTEAD? A SOUND PLAN.

HUH?!

BECAUSE FREDDIE'S IN THE MIDDLE OF A SONG.

EXACTLY. NO MATTER WHAT SORT OF GAG YOU HAD IN MIND, YOU WOULD BE GUARANTEED TO FAIL. I DON'T MEAN TO SOUND RUDE, BUT BEARING IN MIND YOUR CURRENT ABILITIES, YOU WOULDN'T WIN **ANYONE'S** ATTENTION BY JUMPING OUT NOW.

WELL, YEAH. I CAN'T BELIEVE FREDDIE'S ACTUALLY SINGING! MAN, I WISH I COULD SEE THAT!

I'M SURE YOU CAN UNDER-STAND.

AND THIS WAS HIS PLAN:

His name eludes me, though.

H-HOW COOL!

FINE. I'LL LEAVE IT UP TO YOU, MY MAN. CIAO.

AT LAST! A CHANCE TO SAY MY NAME...AND TO HAVE IT **REMEMBERED!**

THEN, WHEN THE PARTY REACHES ITS CLIMAX AND MECHAZAWA BLOWS OUT THE CANDLES, I LEAP FROM THE CAKE AND YELL "HAPPY BIRTHDAY!"

HAPPY BIRTHDAY!

Here

FIRST, I HIDE INSIDE THE BIRTHDAY CAKE.

BUT, NOW THAT I'VE HAD SOME TIME TO THINK ABOUT IT, I'M WORRIED ABOUT HOW WELL IT WILL GO OVER WITH EVERYONE. ONE THING'S FOR SURE, THOUGH--IF THERE WAS AN EARTHQUAKE OR SOMETHING AND I DIED INSIDE THIS CAKE, IT'D BE PRETTY FRICKIN' EMBARRASSING!

WHEN I FIRST HEARD IT, I THOUGHT IT WAS AN EXCELLENT PLAN...

HM?

rrring

ANYWAY, WHAT I NEED TO WORRY ABOUT RIGHT NOW IS MY TIMING. IF I'M OFF BY JUST A SECOND, IT COULD TOTALLY RUIN THE SURPRISE!

I KNOW WHAT YOU'RE THINKING, BUT HEAR ME OUT.

HIS BIRTH-DAY?!

WELL, MECHAZAWA-KUN'S BIRTHDAY IS COMING UP NEXT WEEK...

HE'D MENTIONED THAT HIS BIRTHDAY WAS COMING UP, AND I THINK WE SHOULD HAVE SOME KIND OF CELEBRATION. I'VE BEEN WORKING ON A **PLAN**.

FIRST AND FOREMOST, MECHAZAWA-KUN IS OUR FRIEND.

INDEED, YOUR ROLE WILL BE PARAMOUNT! YOU WILL BRING THE PARTY TO ITS DRAMATIC CONCLUSION, AND AT THE SAME TIME RECEIVE **RECOGNITION** FROM EVERYONE PRESENT!

OH, YES.

IS THERE ANY-THING I CAN DO?

EXACTLY!

I'LL FINALLY HAVE THE CHANCE TO TELL YOU ALL MY NAME?!

WHAT? DID YOU SAY RECOGNITION?! YOU MEAN...

RIGHT NOW, I'M COOPED UP INSIDE A DARK, CRAMPED PLACE. IN OTHER WORDS...

MY NICKNAME IS THE AMERICAN DREAM. UNFORTUNATELY, EVERYONE JUST CALLS ME "HOKUTO'S HENCHMAN."

AND WHY AM I INSIDE THIS CAKE? WELL, IT ALL STARTED WITH SOME ADVICE KAMIYAMA GAVE ME...

ACTUALLY, IT'S A PRETTY BIG CAKE, SO IT'S NOT *THAT* CRAMPED.

INSIDE THIS CAKE.

SURE. WHAT'S UP?

DO YOU HAVE A MOMENT? I WANTED TO ASK YOU SOMETHING.

NO GOOD. IT'S ONLY ONE-WAY.

AND THIS ONE?

WELL...I STILL THINK IT'S ONE HECK OF A DETOUR.

THAT'S WHY THIS ROAD'S BEST. RIGHT?

YEAH, BUT THERE ARE STILL A FEW RULES WE'RE PROBABLY BETTER OFF FOLLOWING.

I DON'T THINK THAT MATTERS MUCH IF WE'RE IN A **TANK**.

YOU REALLY ARE FROM JAPAN, AREN'T YOU?!

YOU'LL BE FINE IF YOU JUST ROLL WITH IT, BOSS. IT'S LIKE THAT OLD SAYING, "OAKS MAY FALL WHEN REEDS STAND THE STORM."

MERCURY, YOU...

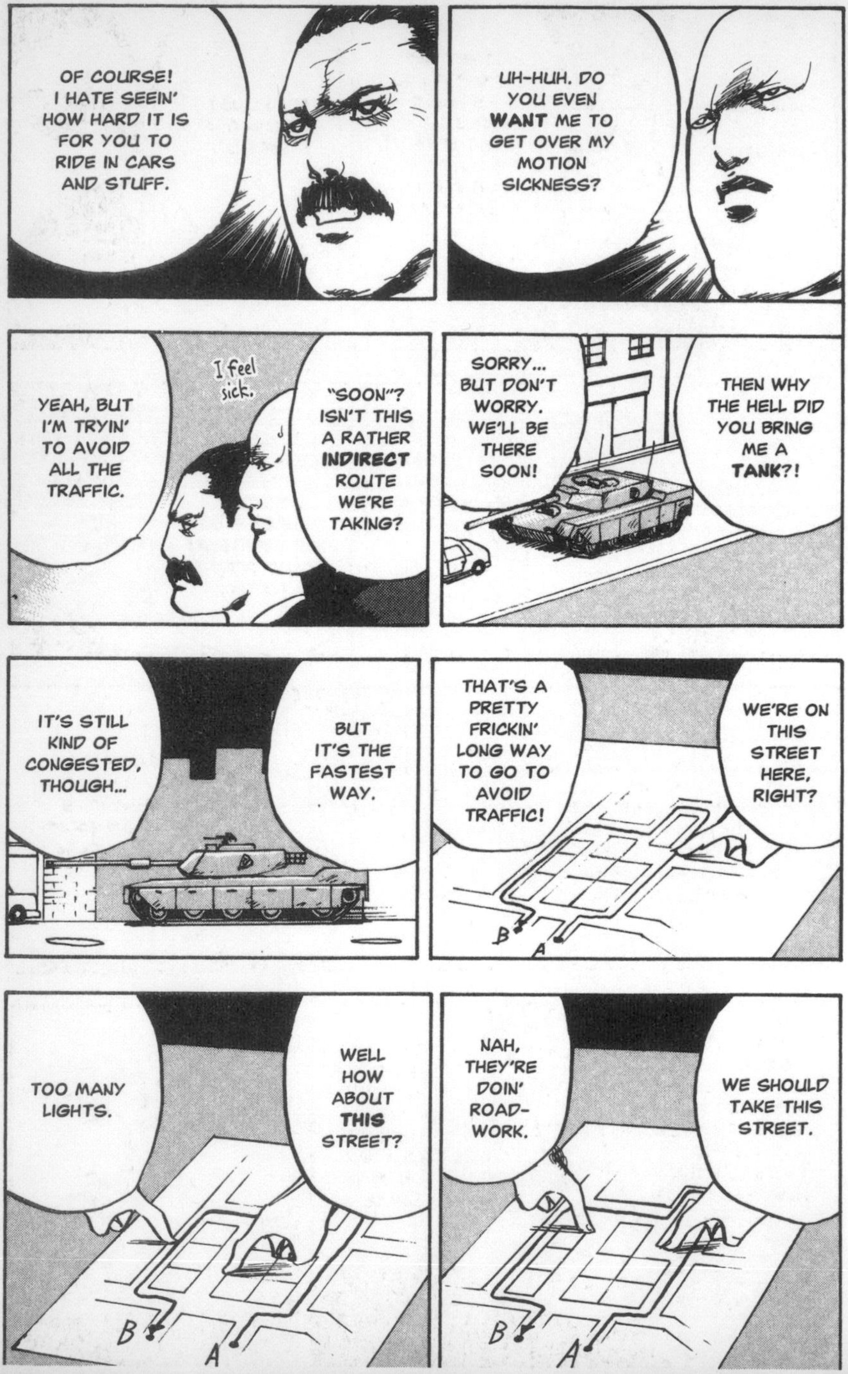
UH-HUH. DO YOU EVEN **WANT** ME TO GET OVER MY MOTION SICKNESS?
OF COURSE! I HATE SEEIN' HOW HARD IT IS FOR YOU TO RIDE IN CARS AND STUFF.
THEN WHY THE HELL DID YOU BRING ME A **TANK**?!
SORRY... BUT DON'T WORRY. WE'LL BE THERE SOON!
"SOON"? ISN'T THIS A RATHER **INDIRECT** ROUTE WE'RE TAKING?
I feel sick.
YEAH, BUT I'M TRYIN' TO AVOID ALL THE TRAFFIC.
WE'RE ON THIS STREET HERE, RIGHT?
THAT'S A PRETTY FRICKIN' LONG WAY TO GO TO AVOID TRAFFIC!
B
A
BUT IT'S THE FASTEST WAY.
IT'S STILL KIND OF CONGESTED, THOUGH...
WE SHOULD TAKE THIS STREET.
NAH, THEY'RE DOIN' ROAD-WORK.
B
A
WELL HOW ABOUT **THIS** STREET?
TOO MANY LIGHTS.
B
A

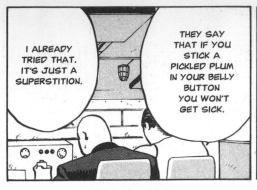

I ALREADY TRIED THAT. IT'S JUST A SUPERSTITION.

THEY SAY THAT IF YOU STICK A PICKLED PLUM IN YOUR BELLY BUTTON YOU WON'T GET SICK.

HEY, I JUST REMEMBERED SOMETHIN'.

YEAH. ESPECIALLY THE FOOD...

YOU MISS IT, HUH?

YOU KNOW, WHEN YOU SAY STUFF LIKE THAT, IT **REALLY** MAKES ME THINK THAT YOU'VE BEEN TO JAPAN.

I ALWAYS FIGURED YOU'D BE HEADIN' BACK HOME SOMEDAY. WHEN THE TIME COMES FOR US TO SAY SAYONARA TO YA, WELL...WE'RE GONNA MISS YOU.

BOSS, I'LL NEVER FORGET THAT TIME YOU SAVED MY BUTT BACK IN BROOKLYN.

YEAH...IT'S A TOUGH ONE. I WANT YOU TO GET OVER YOUR MOTION SICKNESS AND ALL, BUT IF YOU **DO**, YOU'LL JUST HEAD BACK TO JAPAN.

UNTIL I GET OVER THIS MOTION SICKNESS, THERE'S NO **WAY** I CAN GO BACK TO JAPAN.

DON'T WORRY, MERCURY.

BUT BOSS! WITH THIS, WE COULD TAKE 'EM ALL OUT AT ONCE!

IT WOULD'VE BEEN A HELL OF A LOT EASIER TO JUST GO GET A GUN! WHY WOULD YOU... WAIT. YOU'RE DOIN' THIS ON PURPOSE, AREN'T YOU?

GIMME A FRICKIN' BREAK!

I'M SORRY. THIS IS ALL WE HAD...

WELL, AT LEAST YOU TOOK CARE OF THE **DETAILS**...

HEY, NO PROBLEM! I HEAR IF YOU SIT IN THE BACK SEAT, IT'S A LOT HARDER TO GET SICK. AND I BROUGHT YOU SOME PILLS, JUST IN CASE.

YOU'RE THE ONLY ONE I TOLD THAT I CAN'T STAND RIDING IN VEHICLES! IF A TAXI IS ENOUGH TO MAKE ME SICK, WHAT MAKES YOU THINK I CAN RIDE IN A DAMN **TANK**?!

G-CHNK

YEAH, SORRY 'BOUT THAT. BUT THIS THING DRIVES AROUND ON TREADS INSTEAD OF WHEELS, SO IT SHOULDN'T SHAKE TOO MUCH.

BUT CORRECT ME IF I'M WRONG--THIS IS A TWO-SEATER!

YOU WERE SAYING SOMETHING ABOUT A BACK SEAT...

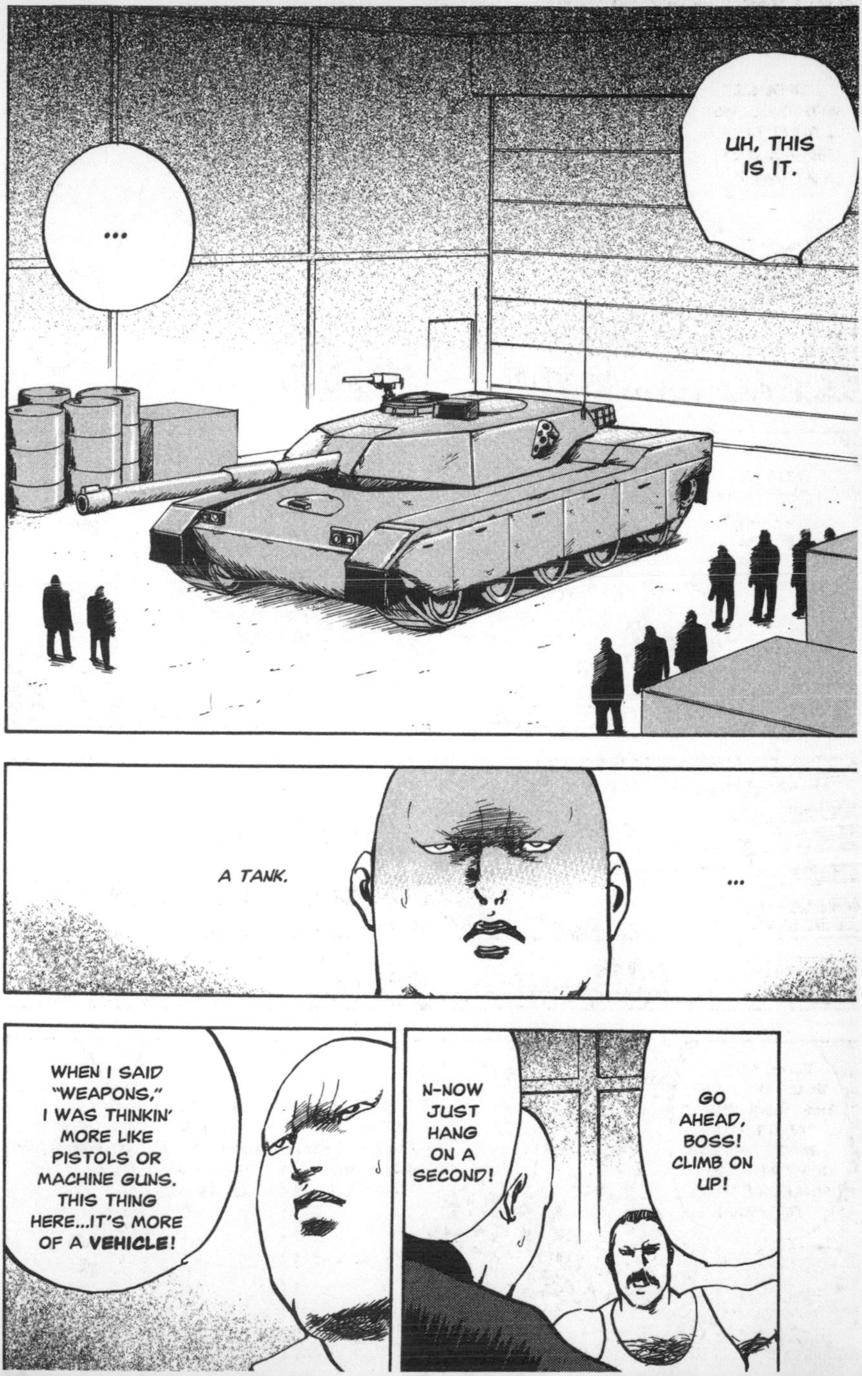
UH, THIS IS IT.
...
A TANK.
...
WHEN I SAID "WEAPONS," I WAS THINKIN' MORE LIKE PISTOLS OR MACHINE GUNS. THIS THING HERE...IT'S MORE OF A VEHICLE!
N-NOW JUST HANG ON A SECOND!
GO AHEAD, BOSS! CLIMB ON UP!

FINE. LET'S JUST DROP IT.

'COURSE NOT! I'M ALL ALONE, MAN! I GOT NO ONE!

WELL, DO YOU HAVE A BROTHER OR SOMETHIN' IN JAPAN?

SIMPLE. WE TURN THE TABLES AND STICK IT TO THEM FIRST!

WHAT'RE WE GONNA DO, BOSS?

WHAT?!

HEY, BOSS! THE DAVIS GANG JUST MOVED ONTO OUR TURF!

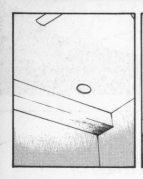

YOU CAN COUNT ON ME.

MERCURY, YOU GO ROUND UP SOME WEAPONS! I WANT EVERYTHING WE'VE GOT. WE'RE GOIN' AFTER THOSE BASTARDS!

WELL? WHERE ARE THEY?

GOOD WORK. LET'S MOVE OUT!

BOSS! I GOT THEM WEAPONS!

CLIMBING SO HIGH IN SUCH A SHORT AMOUNT OF TIME WASN'T EASY, THOUGH. IT'S A GOOD THING I CAN SPEAK ENGLISH (I PASSED LEVEL 1 OF THE ENGLISH PROFICIENCY EXAM). ANYWAY, I'VE GOT A LOT OF GOOD FELLAS UNDER ME NOW...

A LOT SURE HAS HAPPENED ALREADY.

Mr. Mercury.

INCLUDING THIS ONE.

HE GOES BY THE NAME OF MERCURY.

HOW MANY TIMES I GOTTA TELL YA?! LISTEN, BOSS. I AIN'T NEVER BEEN TO JAPAN. I DON'T KNOW A THING ABOUT JAPAN. AND YA KNOW WHAT? I **HATE** JAPAN!

AND I COULD SWEAR THAT I'VE SEEN YOU THERE ONCE OR TWICE.

HEY, MERCURY. I USED TO LIVE IN THIS COUNTRY CALLED JAPAN...

NEW YORK CITY

I'VE BECOME A LEADER IN SOME GROUP CALLED "THE MAFIA," BUT I STILL GET MOTION SICK, SAME AS ALWAYS.

MY NAME IS YUTAKA TAKENOUCHI.

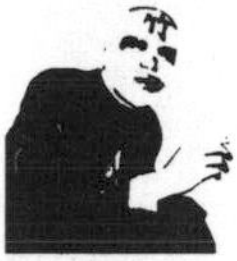

TABLE OF CONTENTS

VALIANTLY FORGING AHEAD! CROMARTIE HIGH SCHOOL 3
"THE BASEBALL STORY." EIJI NONAKA